SCIENCE ADVENTURERS

ANIMAL CONSERVATIONISTS

BY LAURA PERDEW

CONTENT CONSULTANT

Dr. Donald Linzey
Instructional Faculty
Department of Fish and Wildlife Conservation
Virginia Tech

Essential Library

An Imprint of Abdo Publishing
abdobooks.com

ABDOBOOKS.COM

Published by Abdo Publishing, a division of ABDO, PO Box 398166, Minneapolis, Minnesota 55439.
Copyright © 2020 by Abdo Consulting Group, Inc. International copyrights reserved in all countries.
No part of this book may be reproduced in any form without written permission from the publisher.
Essential Library™ is a trademark and logo of Abdo Publishing.

Printed in the United States of America, North Mankato, Minnesota.
092019
012020

THIS BOOK CONTAINS RECYCLED MATERIALS

Cover Photos: iStockphoto (front); Shutterstock Images (back)
Interior Photos: Merlin D. Tuttle/Science Source, 4–5; USFWS/Science Source, 7; Dan Gunderson/Minnesota Public Radio/AP Images, 11; Shutterstock Images, 12–13, 20–21, 48–49; AP Images, 17; Jixin Yu/Shutterstock Images, 23; Andre Penner/AP Images, 24–25; Patrick Lynch/Alamy, 28–29; Gagliardi Photography/Shutterstock Images, 31; JHVE Photo/iStockphoto, 32–33; Jason Ondreicka/iStockphoto, 35; Georgi Baird/Shutterstock Images, 36–37; Nick Ut/AP Images, 40; Eric Watson/Shutterstock Images, 43; Susan Montoya Bryan/AP Images, 45; Eric Risberg/AP Images, 47; Suzette Laboy/AP Images, 51, 54; Rigucci/Shutterstock Images, 57; Jack Smith/AP Images, 58–59, 62; Carl Iwasaki/ The LIFE Images Collection/Getty Images, 60; S.R. Maglione/Shutterstock Images, 65; Michael Male/Science Source, 69; Mauro Pimentel/AFP/Getty Images, 70–71; Susan Schmitz/Shutterstock Images, 74; Herman Verwey/Foto24/ Gallo Images/Getty Images, 76–77; Ivan Kuzmin/Shutterstock Images, 80–81; Arnulfo Franco/AP Images, 83; Thomas Barrat/Shutterstock Images, 87; Lisa Strachan/Shutterstock Images, 89; Wilfredo Lee/AP Images, 90–91; Lenny Ignelzi/AP Images, 93; TEK Image/ Science Source, 95; Joe Mwihia/AP Images, 96–97

Editor: Arnold Ringstad
Series Designer: Laura Graphenteen

LIBRARY OF CONGRESS CONTROL NUMBER: 2019942084

PUBLISHER'S CATALOGING-IN-PUBLICATION DATA

Names: Perdew, Laura, author.
Title: Animal conservationists / by Laura Perdew
Description: Minneapolis, Minnesota : Abdo Publishing, 2020 | Series:
    Science adventurers | Includes online resources and index.
Identifiers: ISBN 9781532190322 (lib. bdg.) | ISBN 9781532176173 (ebook)
Subjects: LCSH: Animal diversity conservation--Juvenile literature. | Wildlife
    conservation--Juvenile literature. | Scientists--Juvenile literature.
    | Discovery and exploration--Juvenile literature. | Adventure and
    adventurers--Juvenile literature.
Classification: DDC 591.90--dc23

CONTENTS

CHAPTER ONE
RACING TO SAVE BATS 4

CHAPTER TWO
THE HISTORY OF ANIMAL
CONSERVATION 12

CHAPTER THREE
SAVING HABITATS,
SAVING SPECIES 24

CHAPTER FOUR
BREEDING AND
REHABILITATION 36

CHAPTER FIVE
AQUATIC BREEDING 48

CHAPTER SIX
REINTRODUCTION 58

CHAPTER SEVEN
TECHNOLOGY IN ANIMAL
CONSERVATION 70

CHAPTER EIGHT
BATTLING INVASIVE SPECIES 80

CHAPTER NINE
THE FUTURE OF ANIMAL
CONSERVATION SCIENCE 90

ESSENTIAL FACTS 100
GLOSSARY 102
ADDITIONAL RESOURCES 104
SOURCE NOTES 106
INDEX 110
ABOUT THE AUTHOR 112

RACING TO SAVE BATS

The cave is darker than night, aside from the sweep of light from headlamps. Water drips into pools on the cave floor and seeps down the walls. The air is heavy and cool. Footsteps echo. It is otherworldly. The cave is a subterranean hideaway, seemingly without life. But, in fact, caves contain complex ecosystems full of life. In many places around the world, caves are also the refuge of millions of bats. In a cave with a healthy ecosystem, the walls are often adorned with bats roosting upside down.

Across the United States there are 47 different species of bats.[1] These small flying mammals have a fast metabolism and are highly intelligent. Bats are also the main predators of flying night insects. They do a remarkable

Vast numbers of bats roost in caves throughout the United States.

There are more than 1,300 species of bats on six continents around the world.[2]

CITIZENS FOR BATS

People do not need a degree in science to help bats. In fact, more and more scientists are asking for the help of citizen scientists. In Wisconsin, for example, volunteers conduct acoustic bat surveys. Bats use echolocation when they fly and hunt, but the noises involved are inaudible to humans. Using special ultrasonic detection equipment, also called "bat detectors," volunteers can help collect data about bats in their area. In Indiana, a different citizen science project collects data on bats' summer roosting locations. Volunteers observe and record the locations and number of colonies, as well as the number of bats in them, throughout the state. The information helps biologists learn more about bats and how disease may affect them. Partnerships between citizens and the professional scientific community are invaluable to conservation.

job of keeping insect populations in check. Bats can be seen flying in large colonies, dotting the dusk and dawn skies.

In 2006, however, white-nose syndrome (WNS) was discovered in a cave in New York State. It is a disease caused by a fungus that is not native to North America. It is an invasive species, one of many threats to the survival of native species. Most likely, the fungus was introduced to the United States from Europe. The disease grows on hibernating bats, appearing as a white mold-like fuzz on bats' noses and wing tissue. Even in hibernation, the bats' bodies fight the disease. Yet this causes them to use the valuable energy they've stored to make it through the winter. As a result, bats with WNS either starve to death in the cave or emerge from hibernation early looking for food. But because it is often still winter, there isn't any food available.

Between the disease's 2006 appearance in the United States and 2019, it spread to 36 US states and seven Canadian provinces, killing entire colonies of bats. Scientists estimate that more than six million bats have died from WNS.[3] There has been great concern that many species of bats could go extinct in North America as a result of the disease.

In Tennessee, the state chapter of the Nature Conservancy raced to save bats. Cory Holliday, the cave program director of that chapter, was on the front lines of the efforts. He said the group uses "the best available science to find practical solutions to problems."[4] He and his team understood that simply documenting the impact of the disease and the decline of bats was not enough. So the group created three goals: execute cave surveys, fund research on the disease, and build an artificial cave. The cave they built was the first designed and engineered artificial hibernation habitat, called a hibernaculum, for bats. The artificial

WNS has devastated bat populations in North America.

cave project will allow the Nature Conservancy to advance research and test different methods of protecting bats from WNS.

The research was a joint effort between the Nature Conservancy, Georgia State University, the US Forest Service, and Bat Conservation International. These groups worked together and tested different ideas. One possible solution to help the bats fight WNS came from Georgia State. Researchers there discovered that a species of bacteria that is native to North America helps keep the WNS fungus from growing. Scientists treated bats with the bacteria before hibernation. These bats survived the winter and were released in May 2015. Promising solutions like this suggest that animal conservationists are making progress against WNS.

AUSTIN BATS

In the 1980s, the bats in Austin, Texas, faced a threat much different from that of the bats battling WNS: people didn't like them. Soon after the Congress Avenue Bridge was expanded in 1982, Brazilian free-tailed bats took up residence among the crevices under the bridge. The people of Austin felt their city had been invaded. Fearing the bats, they called for eradication. That's when Merlin Tuttle stepped in. As a zoologist, ecologist, conservationist, and bat scholar, Tuttle pointed out the ecological value of bats to city officials. He also informed them about the tens of thousands of insects the colony consumed each night. Tuttle used science and education to guide the city's decision. The bats were left alone. Now, more than one million bats migrate back to the Congress Avenue Bridge every year in the spring and stay until fall. They've become a much-loved icon in the city and attract thousands of tourists.

THE SCIENCE OF ANIMAL CONSERVATION

Animal conservation efforts, such as the work to save bats from WNS in North America, require partnerships between many organizations, researchers, and scientists. These scientists come from many disciplines, including wildlife biology, zoology, ecology, environmental science, marine biology, chemistry, and more.

Scientific research has increased our knowledge of many species, the ecosystems in which they live, and the interactions between them. Increased understanding of complex ecosystems and the species within them, as well as humans' impact on them, is important for making the best, most efficient conservation efforts. Scientists also help identify species at risk and gather data about them. The data is used to inform action, legislation, and policies to protect certain species and their habitats. It is also used to plan new research and secure funding. In addition, scientists help raise awareness about endangered species. Together, experts in a variety of disciplines create the foundation for conservation science.

In the 2000s, science has identified many threats to Earth's species. The biggest are pollution, habitat loss and degradation, climate change, invasive species, and overexploitation. Science is critical

As of 2019, WNS continued to spread across the United States at the rate of one state per year.[5]

WILDLIFE BIOLOGISTS

Wildlife biologists are among the many types of scientists involved in conservation. These scientists study and manage animals and the ecosystems in which they live. They may work in a lab conducting experiments, looking for methods of disease control or analyzing genetics. In the field, wildlife biologists collect data about animals and their habitats, including predator and prey relationships, population numbers, and behavior patterns. Wildlife biologists also research the effects of humans on animals and environments. All of this information gives experts a solid base from which to launch informed animal conservation projects.

SCIENCE INFORMS ELEPHANT CONSERVATION

As a result of the demand for ivory for jewelry and other items, elephant populations are in decline. Of the two types of elephants in Africa, savanna elephants have been most widely studied. Forest elephants have received less attention because they live in dense jungles. Research published in 2016 by biologist Andrea Turkalo revealed that their plight may be as bad as, if not worse than, that of their savanna cousins. She found that since 2002, their numbers had declined by 65 percent.[6] Making matters worse, Turkalo's field research revealed that forest elephants reproduce more slowly than most mammals. As a result, it could take a century for them to recover. Her work is a driving force behind education campaigns and the closing of ivory markets.

to understanding the impact of each of these on different species, in addition to finding the best approaches to conserving species. In some cases this involves habitat protection and restoration. Breeding programs at zoos, aquariums, and sanctuaries also help to prevent extinctions and recover species' populations. Other times, species are reintroduced to their native habitat in order to preserve the ecological balance of ecosystems. Ever-improving technology is also employed to monitor species, collect data, analyze DNA, and more. And, as with the bats across North America, science has taken the lead in battling invasive species, including diseases. Every day, animal conservationists work to save Earth's animals from the wide variety of threats they face.

Conservation scientists work in caves, jungles, deserts, and a huge assortment of other environments as they try to protect species.

THE HISTORY OF ANIMAL CONSERVATION

The conservation movement in the United States dates back to the mid-1800s, when people first began to recognize the need to protect wild places from development, especially in the West. Yosemite was set aside as a nature park in 1864. At the time it was managed by the state of California. Yellowstone National Park was dedicated as the world's first national park in 1872. Authors such as Ralph Waldo Emerson and Henry David Thoreau were also important to the early movement, raising awareness through their writing about the need to protect nature. John Muir and others founded the Sierra Club in 1892, with their stated goal being "to do something for wildness and make the mountains glad."[1]

Throughout the history of animal conservation, park rangers, scientists, and ordinary people have helped save at-risk species.

EXTINCTION

Prior to the 1700s, unearthed fossils were explained as the remains of living species. Then Georges Cuvier, a French naturalist, began to study fossils and bones closely. He was meticulous in his work, examining living and lost species of elephants, including mastodons that once roamed North America. Cuvier declared the mastodon a lost species.

As Cuvier continued his work, he discovered other lost species and concluded that there must be even more. The more fossils and bones he studied, the more extinct species he found. As a result of his work, the idea of extinction became accepted science.

"When we try to pick out anything by itself, we find it hitched to everything else in the universe."[4]

— John Muir, conservationist and founder of the Sierra Club, on the connections between living things in nature

Awareness of the need for animal conservation also emerged. Among the species of concern was the bison. Prior to European exploration of the American West, millions of bison roamed the plains. But once settlers arrived, the animals were systematically slaughtered for their fur, skin, and meat. By the middle of the 1800s, their population numbers had plummeted. At the end of the century, bison faced almost certain extinction, with only 325 left in the United States.[2]

William Temple Hornaday—a well-respected taxidermist for the Smithsonian Institution in Washington, DC—heard reports of the diminishing herds. He began to collect information and reported on the state of bison in the West. Ultimately, he brought live bison back to Washington to put on display, which increased public support and funding for the preservation of the bison. His work is credited with saving the species. Hornaday was also the first to curate a comprehensive list of all species "threatened with early extermination."[3] His work laid the foundation for future lists, both nationally and internationally, that identified species at risk.

Through the early 1900s, more public land was put under federal protection, including 230 million acres (93 million ha) protected by President Theodore Roosevelt.[5] The National Park Service was established in 1916, and the US Fish and Wildlife Service was created in 1940 to protect plants and animals as well as their habitats. Despite these efforts, animal conservation was not at the forefront of many Americans' minds until biologist and author Rachel Carson published *Silent Spring* in 1962.

THE BEGINNINGS OF ANIMAL CONSERVATION SCIENCE

When the bald eagle was chosen as the national symbol of the United States in 1782, the bird was found across North America, from Alaska to northern Mexico. By the mid-1900s, the bald eagle was threatened with extinction as a result of hunting and habitat loss.

The word *ecology* was introduced to the world in 1866 by German zoologist Ernst Haeckel.

IUCN RED LIST

The international list of threatened species is called the International Union for Conservation of Nature (IUCN) Red List of Threatened Species. The IUCN Red List was established in 1964 and is today the most comprehensive source of global information about threatened species. It provides data about the status of species, population numbers, habitats, threats, and conservation guidelines. The list is used by governments and conservationists around the world. Of the more than 96,500 species on the list in 2019, more than 26,500 are threatened with extinction.[6]

In 1940, the Bald and Golden Eagle Protection Act was passed, making it illegal to kill, possess, or otherwise harm eagles. But around the same time, scientists developed and marketed a new synthetic pesticide called DDT. The agriculture industry embraced the new chemical and heralded it as a savior to farming. The problem was, DDT didn't just kill insects. People began to notice a decline in bird populations in areas where DDT was sprayed. It was a poison that made its way up the food chain. Birds were among the most affected species. For bald eagles, the pesticide didn't kill them outright. Instead, the poison they ingested when they ate prey contaminated with DDT made their eggshells weak. As a result, eggshells cracked and many eggs did not hatch, resulting in declining eagle populations.

Warnings about the harmful effects of DDT went largely unnoticed and unrecognized. Then, in 1962, *Silent Spring* was published. The title was drawn from a "Fable for Tomorrow" Carson wrote in chapter one, warning that the songs of birds in the springtime would be silenced in a world with uncontrolled pesticide use. *Silent Spring* was the culmination of Carson's exhaustive and thorough scientific

MARTHA'S LEGACY

Around the time Europeans began to settle in North America, the number of passenger pigeons was estimated to be between three and five billion. That represented one quarter of all birds on the continent.[7] By 1900, as a result of unchecked hunting, there were no passenger pigeons left in the wild. Ornithologists and other scientists tried desperately to find more birds in the wild and breed them in captivity. But the efforts were unsuccessful. The last known passenger pigeon in the world was named Martha. She was well cared for at the Cincinnati Zoological Garden until she died at the age of 29 in 1914. On that day, the world watched a species go extinct right before its eyes. Because of this, people were moved to push for stronger conservation laws, and many species since have been saved.

investigation into how DDT affects the environment. It was a call to action. "We must begin to count the many hidden costs of what we are doing," Carson said.[8]

Following the publication of *Silent Spring*, Carson was criticized and threatened by allies of the agriculture and chemical industries. But she was dedicated to informing the American public and was able to stand behind her book. Thanks largely to her work, DDT was banned from use in the United States in 1972. Populations of bald eagles, peregrine falcons, brown pelicans, and other species eventually rebounded. By the end of the century, bald eagles were no longer endangered, and as of 2007 there were close to 10,000 nesting pairs of bald eagles in the contiguous United States.[9]

More broadly, Carson's work initiated a shift in science. Previously, the role of

Rachel Carson played a pivotal role in launching the modern conservation movement.

science had been to triumph over and control nature. Following *Silent Spring*, however, scientists were called on to preserve nature and to ask hard questions about how humans affect the environment. It was the beginning of the modern environmental movement and environmental science. The bald eagle remains not only a national symbol but also a symbol for what science, activists, laws, and determination can achieve in the fight to protect biodiversity.

SILENT SPRING BACKLASH

When Rachel Carson's *Silent Spring* hit the bookstores in 1962, it sold hundreds of thousands of copies. It was also called the year's most controversial book. For many people, the book opened their eyes to the balance of nature and how humans can upset that balance. Others, however, firmly believed that the role of science was to control nature. Carson was called a communist, a hysterical female, and an enemy of technology and progress. From small farmers to large factory farms, the agriculture industry pushed back against Carson's work. The chemical industry claimed that Carson's work was distorted and unscientific. It even went so far as to argue that her work would undermine American agriculture and pose a threat to human health. Yet through it all, Carson defended her work. In doing so, she changed the course of modern conservation science.

THE ENDANGERED SPECIES ACT

The changing public view of conservation was essential for the creation of the Endangered Species Act (ESA) in 1973. Prior to that, lists of endangered animals had done little to actually protect species at risk. Yet conservationists saw the effects of pollution, overexploitation, habitat loss, disease, and invasive species on both animals and plants. Many species had already gone extinct, including the passenger pigeon. And many others were at risk, including the Florida manatee, the American alligator, and the grizzly bear. When President Richard Nixon signed the ESA into law, it became one of the most significant environmental laws in the history of the United States. The goal of the ESA is to protect endangered species and the ecosystems in which they live.

Under the act, species can be listed as either endangered or threatened. It covers mammals, birds, reptiles, amphibians, insects, plants and trees, and marine species. "Endangered species" are those species at risk of becoming extinct in their native habitats; "threatened species" are those likely to become endangered. "Candidate species," or species of concern, are under consideration for listing because scientists have noted population declines. Under the law, federal agencies must avoid any actions that could harm listed species. The law also creates penalties for anyone who harms those species.

The foundation for the protection and recovery of listed species is in science. Scientists in the field work directly to protect, rehabilitate, and breed species, as well as to maintain and restore habitats. They also inform state and federal governments to guide legislation. As of 2019, there were more than 1,400 animal species listed under the ESA (as well as 900 plant species).[10] As a result of the law and the exhaustive work of

WELCOME TO THE ANTHROPOCENE

Geologists have divided the timeline of Earth's history into chunks of time called eras. Each era is further divided into periods, and recent periods are subdivided into epochs. Each time period marks the important events in the history of Earth. Perhaps the best known era is the Mesozoic, the age of the dinosaurs. The current era is the Cenozoic, and the current epoch is the Holocene. Yet geologists, scientists, and other experts debate whether we have entered into a new geologic time period. Since the Industrial Age in the late 1800s, humanity's impact on the environment, and on other species, has increased. These impacts have become so pervasive and permanent that they will be recorded in the geologic record. This new era is called the Anthropocene, meaning the age of man.

scientists in the field, 99 percent of species listed since the ESA went into effect in 1973 are still alive today.[11]

The American alligator was among the species protected by the ESA when the law was first signed.

SCIENCE CONNECTION

BIOMAGNIFICATION

When pesticides, toxins, and other chemicals enter a habitat, they affect not just the soil, air, and water, but also the plants and the animals that live there. The pollutants enter the food chain. For example, in the marine environment, phytoplankton are at the base of the food chain. Pollutants in the environment are naturally taken up by the phytoplankton. Then, small fish and zooplankton eat the phytoplankton. As a result, the toxic chemicals are found in greater concentrations in the small fish and zooplankton. At every link in the food chain, the concentration of toxic chemicals increases. Therefore, the top predators, such as birds and salmon, may accumulate high levels of a toxic chemical that can cause death or deformities. This process is known as biomagnification. This was the plight of the bald eagle in the middle part of the 1900s. The pesticide DDT was biomagnified in these top predators to the point where the eggshells produced by the birds were soft and easily broken.

Plastic pollution has also contributed to this problem. Plastic that enters an ecosystem never decomposes. Instead, it breaks down into smaller and smaller pieces, called microplastics. Not only does the plastic itself carry toxins but it also attracts other toxic substances known as persistent organic pollutants (POPs). POPs are then ingested by marine species and bioaccumulate up the food chain.

SAVING HABITATS, SAVING SPECIES

For species to thrive, they need healthy, productive habitats. Yet in the 2000s, habitat destruction and degradation are among the leading causes of species loss. These losses are a result of urban development, logging and mining, roads, pesticide use, pollution, conversion of land to agriculture, and climate change. Science is guiding conservation efforts through informed habitat restoration and construction, as well as the establishment of protected areas.

Deforestation and other forms of habitat destruction are sometimes plainly visible when they cut sharp lines across natural ecosystems.

The word *ecosystem* first appeared in England in 1935.

HABITAT FRAGMENTATION

Habitat fragmentation has occurred throughout the world. In the Amazon rain forest, rapid and uncontrolled deforestation has resulted in countless isolated and fragmented habitats. To study the impacts of fragmentation on biodiversity, the Biological Dynamics of Forest Fragmentation Project (BDFFP) was founded in 1979 in Brazil. Now called the Amazon Biodiversity Center, it is the largest and longest running conservation research project that studies habitat fragmentation. Among other effects of fragmentation in the rain forest is that there are more edges around each isolated fragment. As a result, instead of a natural, deep, dark forest, more light enters the rain forest, affecting ground cover and the species within the fragment. One of the goals of the Amazon Biodiversity Center is to use the best conservation science to guide land management policy to protect the fragile ecosystem.

THE EVERGLADES

The natural Everglades ecosystem once covered more than 18,000 square miles (46,600 sq km) of central and southern Florida.[1] This complex ecosystem includes many distinct habitats, including hardwood forests, pinelands, mangroves, cypress swamps, saw grass marshes, freshwater sloughs, and ponds. The common thread throughout is water. Historically, a shallow, slow-moving sheet of water flowed across these landscapes and provided habitats for hundreds of species of fish, amphibians, reptiles, mammals, birds, and insects, as well as plants. Some of those species are found nowhere else on Earth.

However, as European settlers moved into the area in the late 1800s, they built canals, levees, and roads, and they filled or drained wetlands so land could be used for agriculture and urban development. Water management and flood control continued unregulated for decades, resulting in a network of disconnected and interrupted habitats. This forever altered the historical hydrology of the ecosystem. This habitat loss and degradation affected the species that lived there, eliminating some 90 percent of the Everglades' nesting bird population.[2]

Finally, in 1947, the efforts of conservationists and activists, including Marjory Stoneman Douglas, resulted in the establishment of Everglades National Park to prevent further degradation and to preserve species. Still, the damage to the greater Everglades ecosystem was not repaired, and urban development in southern Florida continued. The Everglades habitats remained isolated and fragmented, and the hydrology remained altered. Many places in the Everglades no longer received the water needed to sustain habitats and the species that lived there, while other areas held too much water.

Major restoration of the Everglades finally began in the 1980s. The overarching goal was to reestablish as much of the natural hydrology of the ecosystem as possible, while also improving water quality, restoring habitats, and protecting native species. Then, in 2000, the Comprehensive Everglades Restoration

PROTECTED AREAS

Since the establishment of the first national park, Yellowstone, in 1872, the United States has continued to conserve nature by creating protected areas. This strategy has resulted in the protection of millions of acres and is a powerful tool in conservation. As of 2019, the United States had 476,129 square miles (1,233,169 sq km) of protected lands such as national parks, state parks, and national forest and wilderness areas. This accounted for approximately 13 percent of the country's total land.[3] The United States also had more than 1,700 Marine Protected Areas (MPAs).[4] These areas are managed by different agencies with different levels of restrictions on human use and other protections.

"Probably no phenomenon better typifies man's desecration of the southern Florida wilds than the disappearance of the alligator through his unknowledgeable attempts to manipulate nature's plan of watering the Everglades."[5]

—Entomologist F. C. Craighead Sr., 1968

Plan (CERP), developed by scientists, policymakers, and environmentalists, was authorized by Congress. It is the largest watershed restoration effort in the United States. Its timeline spans over 30 years. CERP is made up of dozens of projects, each guided using the best available science to restore the proper amount, quality, and distribution of water through the Everglades.

One such project is called the Fauna Project. Historically, the Everglades experienced a wet season and a dry season. The dry season initiates the mating season for wading birds because smaller pools of remaining water concentrate the birds' prey, making it easier to catch for themselves and their young. However, after the Tamiami Trail, a road that bisects the Everglades, was built in 1928, the typical wet and dry seasons were altered. The part of the Everglades south of the road often dried out completely during

A century of development brought significant harm to the Everglades, but restoration projects have begun to restore the region's habitats.

the dry season because the road acted like a dam, preventing water from flowing into the area. North of the trail there was often too much water, making catching prey much more difficult for nesting birds. To help restore a more normal flow through this part of the Everglades, a series of bridges were built to elevate the road, allowing water to flow under it. But for this project to be successful, scientists needed to determine optimal water levels year-round to reestablish historic flow.

This is where the Fauna Project came in. A group of scientists was charged with determining the optimal water levels for each season in many regions of the Everglades. To do this, they had to collect data. Using airboats or helicopters to get to different hard-to-reach areas of the Everglades, the researchers identified different zones to survey, including some that had optimal water levels. The researchers then slogged through these zones in waders, recording information about water levels and vegetation. They also collected samples of animals to give them information about prey density, abundance, and diversity. The information helped CERP build a model for optimal

AMERICAN ALLIGATOR COMEBACK

Science has revealed the critical role the American alligator plays as a keystone species in the Everglades ecosystem. These reptiles are also considered ecosystem engineers. Alligators create "alligator holes" prior to the dry season; these holes hold water throughout the season, even when much of the ecosystem dries out. The alligator holes are a refuge for many species, and without them some species would not survive.

Yet due to overexploitation and the draining of the Everglades, by the mid-1900s alligator populations had dropped so low that people feared the species would never recover. It was listed as endangered in 1967 and put on the Endangered Species List in 1973. Yet with the ban on hunting and the preservation of the Everglades, Florida is now home to up to two million alligators.[6]

Airboats enable tourists and scientists alike to navigate the waters of the Everglades.

water levels across the Everglades throughout the year to inform the CERP project on how to elevate the Tamiami Trail.

While extensive efforts have been made since the CERP projects were initiated and while more water flows through the Everglades than before the projects began, progress has been slow. Essentially, the program is replumbing a vast ecosystem, and species are not recovering as quickly as once hoped. Funding continues to be an issue, and scientists are

also concerned about the effects of climate change and rising sea levels. That said, in 2017 and 2018, the strong number of nesting wading birds, which are critical indicator species in the Everglades, provides hope that the ecosystem is recovering.

BUTTERFLY HABITATS

Habitat protection and restoration are also important for the monarch butterfly. Monarchs are native to North America, and historically millions made an epic migration from the United States and Canada to winter in Mexico every year. Throughout the winter, the oyamel fir forests north of Mexico City were adorned with as many as 700 million monarch butterflies. Yet as of 2019, scientists reported that the eastern monarch population had declined by more than 80 percent since the 1980s. The western population that winters in California had declined by more than 99 percent.[7]

Monarch butterflies use plants, including trees, in their migration, making conservation a complex challenge.

The major threats to monarch butterflies include habitat loss and degradation due to the destruction of milkweed for crops. Milkweed is the monarch's breeding habitat. Pesticide use, logging, and climate change have also affected the monarch's habitat. Conservation efforts are now ongoing, including protecting remaining monarch habitat, planting milkweed, running monarch captive-breeding programs, and educating the public about gardening to support butterfly populations. One effort in Mexico is focused on creating new habitats for wintering monarch butterflies as climate change threatens existing ones. The plan involves moving trees.

Cuauhtémoc Sáenz-Romero, a forest geneticist in Morelia, Mexico, has seen the effect of climate change on oyamel fir trees, which serve as the monarchs' wintering grounds. He estimates that the habitat of the oyamel fir trees will shrink 70 percent between 2025 and 2035 as a result of rising temperatures. In response, Sáenz-Romero decided to relocate the forest to a higher altitude. To keep up with climate change, Sáenz-Romero and other scientists began relocating oyamel fir trees 1,300 feet (400 m) up the hill in the Monarch Butterfly Biosphere Reserve.[8] When planting the seedlings, the team made sure the young trees

POLLINATOR GARDENS

Butterflies and other pollinators are getting help from everyday people who are joining the conservation effort. Many pollinators, including butterflies and bees, are in decline as a result of habitat loss and degradation. So people are planting gardens and creating landscapes that support pollinators at home, at work, and in the community. Part of this effort includes educating the public about the need for such gardens and about the types of flowers and plants pollinators prefer. This includes planting milkweed and nectar plants specifically for monarch butterflies.

were shaded by nearby bushes to protect them from sun and harsh temperatures.

Since 2017, Sáenz-Romero and his team have shifted more than 750 seedlings.[9] As of 2019, the results were encouraging, but they need to gather more data about the oyamel firs and the conditions needed for them to thrive. They hope to someday plant the trees at even higher altitudes on other mountains close by. The tree-moving project may seem monumental, but Sáenz-Romero knows that's what needs to be done to protect the monarch butterflies.

Milkweed is crucial to the monarch's life cycle.

CHAPTER FOUR

BREEDING AND REHABILITATION

O ften species at risk of extinction can no longer thrive and maintain a stable population in the wild. When scientists identify such species, helping the animals may involve a captive breeding and rehabilitation program. This human intervention can prove crucial in preventing an animal's extinction.

THE STORY OF THE CALIFORNIA CONDOR

Historically, California condors were found all along the Pacific coast from southern California north to British Columbia, Canada. By the late 1930s, however, there were no condors reported outside of California. The birds

The California condor is at the center of one of the most well-known modern American conservation success stories.

California condors are the largest birds in North America. Their wingspan is 9.5 feet (2.9 m), and they can weigh as much as 25 pounds (11 kg).[2]

ROCKY MOUNTAIN RAPTOR PROGRAM

Some animal conservation programs don't actively breed animals. Instead, they work to rehabilitate injured animals brought in from the wild. The Rocky Mountain Raptor Program (RMRP) in Colorado rescues, rehabilitates, and releases injured raptors. Birds of prey are injured by electric lines, hunters, traps, cars, and more. When these birds are brought in, veterinary experts and volunteers first calm and assess them. Then the birds are treated for their injuries, fed, and nurtured in small cages to restrict movement and prevent further injury. Once a bird is strong enough, it is moved to a larger cage where it can begin to practice flying again and regain strength. Of the approximately 300 birds brought to the RMRP each year, 80 percent of the treatable birds are released back into the wild.[3]

were considered endangered by 1967, and scientists began studying the reasons for their decline. By 1982, there were only 22 California condors left.[1]

Biologists discovered that, in addition to suffering from other human impacts, the birds were dying from lead poisoning. California condors are scavengers that feed on the carcasses of dead animals. As settlers moved across North America, they increasingly left behind animal carcasses shot with lead bullets. When a condor ingests lead fragments from bullets, the toxic element is absorbed into the bloodstream and is pumped into many organs and tissues, including the brain and even bones. If a condor ingests too much lead, it affects the bird's motor function and neural connections.

In an effort to recover the population of condors, the US Fish and Wildlife Service began a captive breeding program in 1983 in partnership with the Los Angeles Zoo and the San Diego Wild Animal Park. In the wild, though, numbers continued to decline.

In 1987, the decision was made to capture the few remaining wild California condors in a last-ditch effort to save the species.

The rate of reproduction proved to be another obstacle to recovering the condor population. California condors do not reproduce until age six, and then they typically lay only one egg per year. To address this in captivity, the caretakers removed eggs as they were laid, which usually caused the condor to lay a second or even a third egg. The removed eggs were incubated and raised by humans wearing a hand puppet that looked like a condor head so the young birds would not imprint on people. By 1987, the recovery program had 177 captive birds.[4]

Decades later, in 2017, scientists also discovered that one of their captive female birds, Anyapa, turned out to be a good surrogate mom. She doesn't have a mate, and usually condors will not raise a chick without a partner. However, she does have a close bond with one of the human caretakers. One season when there was an extra egg at the Los Angeles Zoo, they gave it to Anyapa. She was so good at being a mom, they gave her a second egg. Anyapa tenderly cared for both chicks, and they thrived. This was a breakthrough for the conservation efforts of the California condor.

CRITICS OF CAPTIVE BREEDING

While captive breeding programs have proven successful in recovering populations of endangered species, not everyone thinks it's a good idea. To start, critics cite genetic diversity as a major issue, stating that with severely affected species, genetic diversity among the remaining individuals may be too low to regenerate a viable population. They also maintain that natural habitats may be too severely degraded or gone to ever return a species to the wild. Critics also believe that efforts to save species focus on only a few well-known species and that successful efforts give a false sense of hope that the race against extinction is being won. Finally, they contend that the extraordinary cost of such programs may divert funds from other conservation efforts.

Conservationists have worked hard for decades to rescue the California condor from extinction.

The efforts to reestablish the California condor, and scientists' growing understanding of the birds, has been ongoing. The first captive-bred condors were released back into the wild in California in 1992. Jan Hamber, one of the scientists who helped capture the final condors on Easter Sunday 1987, said, "I've waited for this minute for five years. We're the ones who were here when the last ones were brought in. It's just incredibly exciting to see the birds come back into the wild."[5] Since then, releases have occurred yearly in California, the Baja Peninsula of Mexico, and Arizona. The goal of the program is to establish two geographically distinct populations, each with 150 condors, that are self-sustaining. A third population will remain in captivity. As of 2018, the total number of California condors was more than 400.[6] Even more importantly, the first wild condor chick hatched in April 2018.

While biologists have determined that the wild condors have enough food, water, and shelter, monitoring efforts reveal that they are still at risk for lead poisoning. During the 2015–2016 season, biologists found that 29 percent of the condors they monitored needed treatment for lead poisoning, and as much as 73 percent had lead levels that implied recent exposure.[7] The science is clear that lead bullets poison California condors and other species, but legislation to ban such bullets has been slow to catch up. The use of lead bullets in condor territory in

PROGRAM COSTS

The California Condor Recovery Program has been a success, and today condors are surviving in the wild. But the effort has come at a cost. Between 1987 and 2009 alone, the program cost more than $35 million.[8] Critics of captive breeding programs question whether the investment is worth it. The money is used to pay wildlife biologists, conduct research, house and feed the animals, and monitor released animals. In the case of the California condor, funding was also used to train the birds to avoid power lines after release.

California has been banned since 2007. Many states have laws restricting the use of lead bullets in some circumstances, but conservationists continue to raise awareness among hunters and push for stronger legislation.

ANIMAL MATCHMAKING

The California Condor Recovery Program is just one of hundreds of captive breeding programs in the world. Like the condor program, many are run by partnerships between local and federal agencies. Zoos and aquariums, as well as wildlife sanctuaries, also play a critical role in species recovery and the complicated scientific process of captive breeding.

In order to have a stable and healthy population of animals, there must be genetic diversity. With only a few animals to work with in zoos and aquariums, though, genetic diversity is low, and inbreeding is a risk. This led zoos to start an animal matchmaking program. Zoos in North America have a database that includes the genetic makeup of individual animals. The software for the animal matchmaking was developed by Bob Lacy, a geneticist at the Chicago Zoological Society, and his colleagues. A computer algorithm rates the genes of each animal by how rare they are, and thus how desirable they are in order to maintain all genetic lines in the captive species. The algorithm allows biologists such as Amanda Lawless of the Lincoln Park Zoo in Chicago to look at the lineage of each animal and

Even dog populations need genetic diversity. Purebred dogs are in danger of inbreeding, and diversity is declining. Some scientists are working to raise awareness among breeders to increase diversity and animal health.

The Lincoln Park Zoo is among the facilities working on genetic matchmaking as part of their conservation efforts.

determine ideal matches to ensure genetic diversity. Then, in a planning meeting, the ages of individuals and their temperaments are discussed. If there's a match, the moving vans come. A female rhino made the trip from Kansas to Chicago; a marmoset monkey was transferred from Omaha, Nebraska, to Chicago; and a warthog left Chicago to meet its prospective mate in Maryland. Then everyone waits to see whether the pairs will breed.

FORENSIC GENETICS

In animal conservation, genetics is not just being used in breeding programs. It is also being used to help track down wildlife traffickers. The trafficking of live animals or animal parts is a threat to many species. Now, thanks to advances in science and technology, forensic genetics is being used in wildlife crime cases to identify both the animal and criminal, similarly to how it is used in solving human crime cases. For example, if a shipment of animals or animal parts is seized by authorities, scientists can determine the species and where they came from. Wildlife authorities can also collect animal blood and hair samples from a hunter's vehicle if the hunter is suspected of killing an animal illegally. The evidence is used in court to prosecute criminals and to aid wildlife protection and conservation efforts.

If populations of animals recover enough in captivity, zoos sometimes reintroduce them into the wild. Such was the case with the Mexican gray wolf. By the 1980s, the species was almost extinct in the wild. The US Fish and Wildlife Service captured the remaining seven animals, hoping the species could be saved. Zoos used the matchmaking software on the wolves. As of 2019, there were more than 200 Mexican gray wolves, and many had been released into the wild.[9] The Association of Zoos and Aquariums (AZA) has played a role in numerous species recovery programs, including the condor, the Mexican gray wolf, black-footed ferrets, freshwater mussels, and the Oregon spotted frog. All of its work is performed by a team of dedicated people using up-to-date science.

Public pressure can play a role in animal conservation. In 2012, people protested at a US Fish and Wildlife Service regional headquarters in New Mexico in support of releasing more Mexican gray wolves.

SCIENCE CONNECTION

GENETICS

Genes carry traits that are passed down from parents to offspring; these traits affect behavior and physical appearance. The differences in behavior and appearance between individuals within a single species are due to genetic diversity. The greater the genetic diversity, the better the species will be able to adapt to environmental changes. If there is low genetic diversity, however, it is less likely that a species will survive in the wild.

Knowledge of genetics is helping to recover species populations, both within captive breeding populations and in small populations in fragmented habitats. In conservation genetics, scientists must first understand how individuals are related within a species population. To do this, geneticists gather DNA samples. These samples can be collected from blood, hair, skin, bones, or saliva. Scientists use software to analyze the DNA sequences, comparing the sequences with those of other individuals in a genetic database. The sequences of chemicals in DNA determine the traits that an organism will have.

In captive breeding programs, this is when the matchmaking comes in to ensure the best genetic diversity. In the wild, biologists look at isolated populations that may be experiencing inbreeding and introduce a new animal with strong genetic diversity.

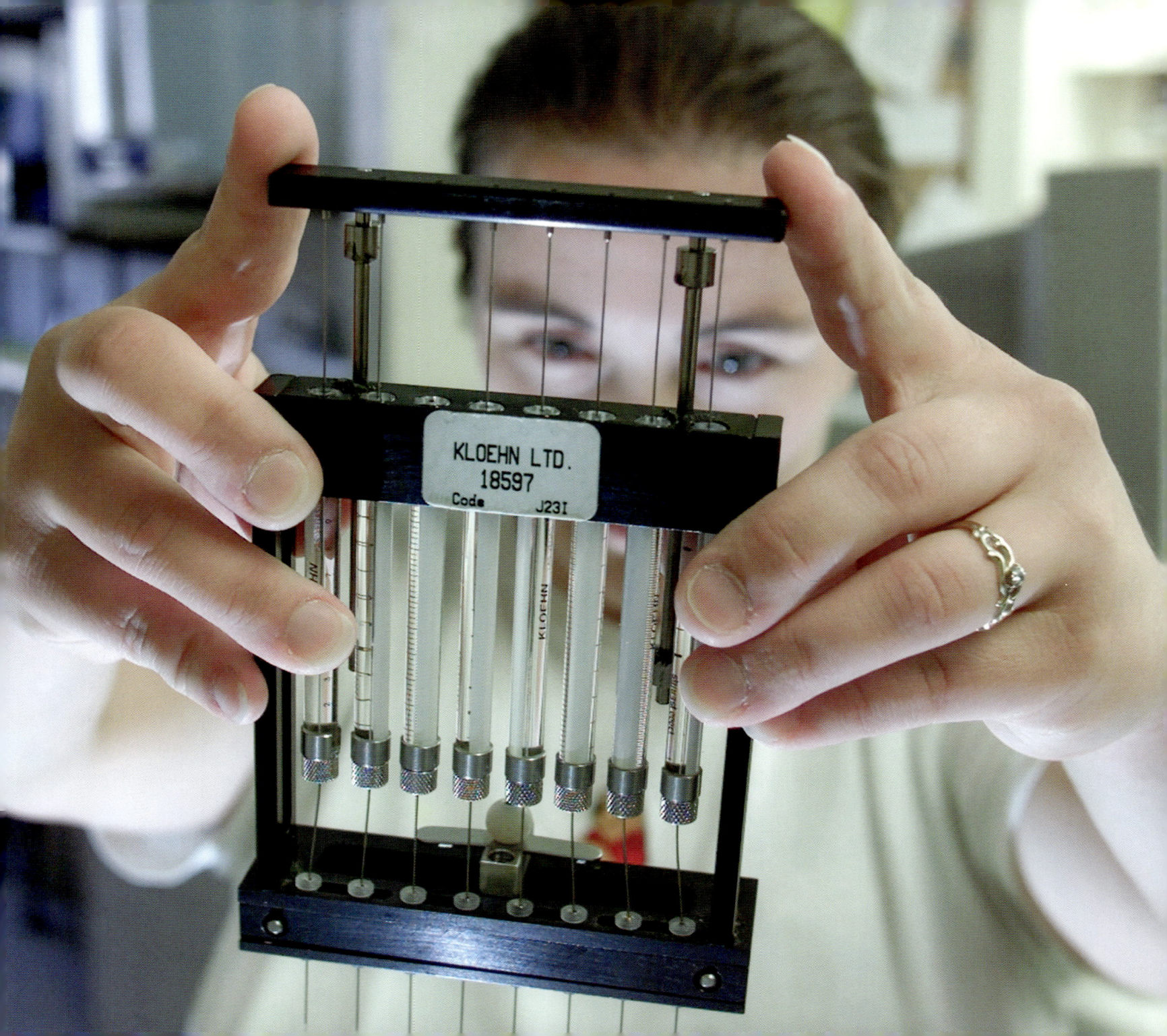

AQUATIC BREEDING

Breeding programs are not just for terrestrial species. Advances in science have led to an increasing number of breeding programs in aquatic environments. Among the ecosystems targeted by these programs are coral reefs.

Coral reefs are found in tropical oceans around the world. Reefs provide food and shelter for 25 percent of marine species, and they protect shorelines from storms, flooding, and erosion.[1] They are considered the backbone of tropical ocean ecosystems. Yet in the 2000s, scientists are warning that the health of the world's coral reefs is rapidly declining as a result of climate change, pollution, and other human activities.

Coral reefs are among the world's most beautiful and at-risk ecosystems.

CORAL RESTORATION

The Great Barrier Reef off the coast of Australia is the largest reef in the world, spanning 1,200 miles (1,930 km). It started growing approximately 20,000 years ago.[2]

Coral reefs are made up of millions of individual corals. They may look like plants or rocks, but they are actually animals. These marine invertebrates range in size from as small as a pinhead to larger than a basketball. Corals grow together to create colonies. Over centuries, they connect with other colonies to create reefs that may be hundreds of miles long.

Ken Nedimyer witnessed firsthand the decline in corals in the Florida Keys over several decades. Then one day in the late 1990s, he noticed some critically endangered corals growing on rocks, not on a reef. That got him thinking. Nedimyer and his daughter conducted a science experiment. Could they create a coral nursery, grow the corals, and then transplant them to help damaged reefs? Could coral reefs be actively restored?

In 2003, the father-daughter duo got a permit to transplant six corals onto Molasses Reef, which is near Key Largo. They attached the corals to the ocean floor using a special glue and methods employed by aquarium hobbyists. Those original six multiplied into thousands of corals. In 2007, Nedimyer founded the Coral Restoration Foundation (CRF) and began cultivating more corals to transplant onto the reefs. After experimenting with different methods of growing corals, Nedimyer and his team found that using a tree structure yielded the best results. The tree structures have one main trunk anchored to

Nedimyer, *left*, turned coral restoration from an experiment into an ongoing conservation program.

the ocean floor and many perpendicular branches. Up to 100 coral fragments are hung from these branches.[3] Hanging the corals keeps them up off the sand, which is important to keeping them clean as the corals grow. Nedimyer says, "They seem to grow faster, they don't get disease, they just do so much better."[4] As of 2019, the CRF had seven different offshore coral nurseries, cultivating 11 different coral species.[5]

The Coral Restoration Foundation made history in 2009 when its nursery-raised corals spawned naturally after being replanted. It was the world's first documented case of this happening.

Nedimyer now considers himself a farmer. He knows the best time of year to plant corals and the best time of year to harvest. He starts by collecting small coral fragments; those fragments are then attached to trees in the coral nursery offshore. In six to nine months, the fragments grow large enough to be planted on carefully selected sites of the reef. The CRF has planted more than 74,000 corals off the coast of Florida since 2012.[6] Its focus is on staghorn and elkhorn corals because they are the main reef-building corals and have the best potential to make a difference. "[These] main structure-building corals . . . those are the ones that are in the most trouble and those are the ones that have the most potential to recover," says Nedimyer.[7]

Maintaining genetic diversity in any species is critical for its long-term survival. The same is true for corals. This diversity allows the coral to adapt to changing environments because some individuals will have traits that make them better suited to handle the changes. Without genetic diversity, the corals are less likely to survive environmental changes. Therefore, to build strong reefs, the CRF needed to ensure that the corals it transplanted were genetically diverse. As a result, the coral nurseries are now a source of genetic diversity for corals and are considered genetic banks. Some species that are no longer living in the wild can be found only in these genetic banks.

Scientists continually study these corals, collecting and cataloging information just as biologists at zoos and aquariums do. This information allows researchers to determine how different coral individuals grow. It guides the methods for planting genetically diverse corals, fostering healthy, stable populations of corals in the ocean. The ultimate goal, according to Nedimyer, is not to replant every reef but to foster these healthy, stable populations of corals so they reproduce on their own. In time, the corals themselves can rebuild the reefs.

MONITORING

Monitoring coral growth in vast areas of the ocean is time-consuming, but it is necessary to understand and optimize the best growing conditions for the various types of corals. A lot of that work is done by researchers in wet suits with scuba gear underwater. They swim from site to site

THE FATHER OF OCEAN SCIENCE

While not a formally trained scientist, Jacques Cousteau is considered the father of modern oceanic science. He was born in France in 1910 and had a lifelong love of the water. As an adult, Cousteau wanted to develop a way for humans to stay underwater longer. In 1943, along with engineer Émile Gagnan, Cousteau invented a device called the Self-Contained Underwater Breathing Apparatus, or scuba for short. This opened up the world of sea exploration. He continued to dive and explore while also inventing many other tools for oceanographers. Cousteau also experimented with underwater filmmaking. Throughout the course of his lifetime, Cousteau produced more than 100 documentaries for television, bringing the wonders of ocean exploration to the world.

The CRF trains divers on how to clean coral and ensure that it is planted correctly.

gathering data and recording it on special underwater clipboards with pencils. The CRF also now uses new image processing technology and underwater cameras in its data collection to map out reef sites. Using the images, the CRF stitches together photomosaics of reefs. Then its experts compare the growth of corals at different sites. This process is efficient and reduces the underwater time needed to collect data. Through the ongoing research, the CRF hopes to understand why some coral locations have a higher survival rate for replanted corals than others. The imaging also helps to track the health of the transplanted corals as well as the changes to reefs over time.

Scientists are working to gain a more comprehensive understanding of the factors that affect the success of coral restoration. In addition, this information can be used to identify possible future restoration sites. The CRF's work is driven by research and hard data. This allows it to increase the efficiency and success of its coral transplants. In time, its data collection will add to the bank of scientific knowledge about oceans and coral reefs.

RESTORING FISH POPULATIONS

Restoring a species' population does not always mean directly fostering breeding. In fact, in the case of many fish, restoring populations means getting out of the way. For hundreds of years, humans have dammed, diverted, drained, and otherwise destroyed waterways without understanding the negative effects of these actions. Yet biologists have learned that these waterways are crucial to breeding for millions of migrating fish.

Salmon, sturgeons, steelhead trout, and other species of fish migrate back to where they were spawned in order to reproduce. Many swim thousands of miles. But often human-made barriers block their

NOISE POLLUTION

Anyone who's ever been underwater understands the quiet and tranquility below the surface. That is the natural habitat of marine creatures. Yet in the modern world, that peace is increasingly interrupted by boat noise and offshore drilling. Scientists are now discovering the impacts of noise pollution on fish, marine mammals, and more.

Studies have shown that boat noise slows down the development of sea slugs. It causes stress in spiny lobsters. It interrupts the natural calling and hunting patterns of whales and dolphins. And scientists have learned that a noisy environment makes it harder for fish to learn to fear and avoid the scent of a predator.

As a result of dam building and other human impacts, Atlantic salmon populations are less than half of 1 percent of what they once were.[9]

WHALE EARWAX

Scientists have been known to study strange things in the pursuit of knowledge. Among those strange things is the earwax of whales. Whales, along with other marine mammals, produce earwax just as humans do. By studying the earwax of whales, scientists can learn a lot about not only the whale but also the health of oceans.

In whales, the buildup of earwax actually creates a plug in the ear canal. Instead of impeding hearing, though, this plug acts as a hearing aid. The plug matches the density of water, allowing sound to travel through the ear canal unimpeded. Studying the layers of earwax allows scientists to learn more about a whale's history. It reveals stress levels related to mating. And it shows exposure to pesticides and other pollutants. With advances in technology, scientists hope their whale earwax collection will open up new research possibilities and provide even more data.

journey. If they cannot reach their destinations, they don't spawn and their populations decline.

Knowing this, the National Oceanic and Atmospheric Administration (NOAA) and other organizations evaluate each situation. Every barrier poses a unique challenge to different fish populations. Near Plymouth, Massachusetts, for example, Town Brook empties into Cape Cod Bay. It is also the spawning habitat of river herring. But by the early 2000s, the natural flow of the 1.5-mile (2.4 km) brook was blocked by several dams and other barriers, reducing the number of fish migrating from close to one million to only 150,000 every year.[8] Starting in 2002, the town of Plymouth, NOAA, and other organizations began the first of seven projects to provide passage for the returning river herring. In addition to removing several dams and lowering one dam by 12 inches (30 cm), workers installed fish ladders in two places to create a safe passage around the dam. These ladders are more like slightly inclined stairs filled with water; the fish can then swim or jump each step, bypassing the dam.

NOAA has completed more than 600 fish migration projects, opening up 6,000 miles (9,600 km) of waterways.[10] The efforts are supporting fish populations that have been in decline as a result of barriers. When humans get out of the way, fish can reach their natural breeding grounds and populations can recover.

Fish ladders are one way conservationists can support fish populations that are affected by human development on rivers.

CHAPTER SIX

REINTRODUCTION

There are some species that may not be extinct in the wild but are no longer living throughout their normal range due to habitat destruction, overexploitation, and other factors. These species are considered extirpated in certain areas. Science has shown that the loss of a species in an ecosystem has effects that ripple throughout that ecosystem. As a result, there are numerous programs that assess, plan, execute, and monitor the reintroduction of extirpated species to their natural range.

LYNX REINTRODUCTION IN THE ROCKIES

Prior to European settlement in the American West, the Canada lynx's range extended across Canada and Alaska, south through the Rocky Mountains, and into southern Colorado. Once settlers discovered the lynx in the West in the 1800s, they began trapping the animals for their fur. The trapping

A lynx reintroduction program in Colorado overcame challenges along the way to achieve success.

Human development and hunting reduced the Colorado lynx population to a vanishingly small number.

continued unregulated into the 1900s. In Colorado, people saw fewer and fewer lynx.

Logging and increased development further decreased the lynx population in the West. The lynx was finally put on the Colorado Endangered Species list in 1973, and trapping the lynx became illegal. In 1974 a skier in Colorado spotted a lynx from a chairlift. He returned to the area later to trap the lynx. It was the last known lynx in the state.

Decades later, people at the Colorado Division of Wildlife (DOW), which is now known as Colorado Parks and Wildlife (CPW), had an idea. If humans were responsible for extirpating the lynx from Colorado, could humans also bring them back? The members of the DOW pondered that question. They felt they had the knowledge to reestablish the lynx in Colorado—to return the ecosystem to the way nature had intended.

They began by assembling a team of researchers and biologists from the DOW. Next, they put together a conservation strategy with other agencies, including the US Fish and Wildlife Service, the National Forest Service, and the National Park Service, that outlined steps needed to establish a viable population of lynx in the southern Rockies. This strategy relied on research to understand both the behavior of the lynx and the habitat where the team would reintroduce the lynx. As the team narrowed down potential release areas, it looked for the largest roadless areas in the state, as well as areas with a combination of low human density and high densities of snowshoe hares, the lynx's main prey.

REINTRODUCTION REACTION

While scientists and conservationists understand the need to reintroduce species to their native habitats, sometimes communities fight against reintroductions, especially when they involve carnivores. Ranchers worried about lynx attacking their chickens and sheep. There was also concern that the reintroduction would cause further headaches or restrictions on grazing cattle on public lands. Likewise, loggers and the ski industry were concerned about land- use restrictions protecting the lynx habitat. The DOW also heard from animal rights activists who expressed ethical concerns about the plan, citing the potential harm and suffering of lynx.

After years of planning and preparation, the first lynx of the program was trapped alive and unharmed in 1999 in British Columbia, Canada. Trapping lynx can be challenging. The animals are stealthy by nature, colored like the surrounding snow and able to slink silently along to surprise their prey. Some researchers dangle shiny CDs, coated in beaver scent, near traps. The glint from the rotating CD draws the animals in. Then, the scientists

After reintroducing lynx to Colorado, researchers monitored them carefully to assess how well they were doing.

hope the lynx gets caught in the trap. When the team in British Columbia caught one, the lynx was sedated and evaluated by a veterinarian to assess her health. In other locations, four more lynx were trapped and evaluated. All were headed to Colorado.

They were transported by truck to the Frisco Creek Wildlife Rehabilitation Center in Del Norte, Colorado, where the lynx reintroduction team anxiously awaited their arrival. After a short stay, the five newest Colorado residents were examined once again, and blood was taken for future DNA studies. Each lynx was photographed, prepared for release, and fitted with a radio collar in order to monitor its movements.

At first, though, the mortality rate for the reintroduced lynx was high. Several of the first lynx died of starvation. The reintroduction team studied the situation and assessed the release procedures. The original procedure included only a few days or a week at the rehabilitation facility before release in order to minimize human contact. The team changed this to a minimal three-week stay to give the animals time to fatten up and get acclimated to the high elevation.

In time, the survival rate of reintroduced lynx improved. Yet if they were to reestablish a viable population of lynx in Colorado, the released animals not only had to survive and establish home ranges but also needed to reproduce. The lynx were closely monitored. Finally, four years after the first lynx were

The lynx reintroduction program in Colorado was such a success that other wildlife biologists from around the world used the program as a model. This included a team in Spain working to reintroduce the Iberian lynx.

brought back to Colorado, the team discovered a den with two kittens. A few days later, they discovered another den with two more kittens, then another. In all, the reintroduction team found six dens with a total of 16 kittens.[1] Years later, many of those kittens had litters of their own.

Between 1999 and 2006, 218 lynx made the unique journey from the dense boreal forests of Canada and Alaska to the mountains of Colorado.[2] By 2009, there were 116 documented lynx kittens born in Colorado.[3] There were likely other dens and more kittens that the lynx team hadn't discovered. In 2010, the lynx reintroduction program in Colorado was considered a success. The work of the DOW switched from reintroduction to management and monitoring.

LOUISIANA BLACK BEARS

David Soileau of the US Fish and Wildlife Service's Louisiana Ecological Services Office has many roles. Among them is bear biologist. Louisiana black bears were on the brink of extinction as a result of habitat loss, largely due to agriculture. Soileau worked with private landowners to protect or restore the bears' native habitat. In addition, he has played a critical role in reintroducing the Louisiana black bear to areas without bears that had historically supported populations. He's helped return 48 adult females and 104 of their cubs. As of 2016, he says, "Ongoing research suggests that bears are now abundant in this area."[4]

REINTRODUCTION WORKS

The lynx reintroduction program in Colorado is just one of many programs in the United States and around the world working to reestablish animals in their natural range. One of the best publicized examples was the gray wolf reintroduction into Yellowstone National Park. As with the lynx, wolves were killed for their pelts as Europeans settled in the West. Hunters killed them because they were considered dangerous and predatory. Even park rangers at the time

The success of the lynx proved that careful reintroduction efforts can succeed.

BEAVERS RETURN TO BRITAIN

Four hundred years after beavers were driven to extinction in Britain, they are back. In 2018, a pair of Eurasian beavers was reintroduced to the Forest of Dean in western England. Scientists on the project believe that the return of beavers to the area will increase biodiversity since beavers are ecosystem engineers. Their dams create ponds and ditches, which are ideal habitats for other species. In addition, since beaver dams improve wetland functions, scientists believe that downstream flooding can be reduced. They will monitor the ecological and hydrological benefits of returning the beavers to the area. Michael Gove, Britain's environment secretary, said, "This release is a fantastic opportunity to develop our understanding of the potential impacts of reintroductions."[7]

Some successful reintroductions in the United States include the Pacific fisher to the mountains of Washington State, the black-footed ferret to Badlands and Wind Cave National Parks in South Dakota, and the nene to Hawai'i Volcanoes National Park in Hawaii.

took part in eradicating wolves from Yellowstone to protect ranchers' livestock. The last two wolves in the park were killed in 1926.[5]

In time, however, wildlife experts came to understand the importance of wolves to maintaining a healthy ecosystem in Yellowstone. They were part of the natural web of life there. Wildlife experts put together a reintroduction strategy and released the first wolves to the park in the mid-1990s. Today there are more than 100 wolves in the park living in several different packs.[6]

A lesser-known reintroduction was of the pupfish in Arizona. A hardy species, the pupfish can survive in extremely hot or cold water and in water that is highly acidic or salty. Despite this, it was put on the Endangered Species List in 1986 as the result of a loss of habitat due to groundwater pumping and competition with invasive species. To address the growing concern, park staff at Organ Pipe National Monument in Arizona drained a pond themselves. Then they removed the invasive species and saved the pupfish. The fish were reintroduced after the pond was refilled, and now there are several thousand of them thriving in the area.

PRZEWALSKI'S HORSE

Przewalski's horse in Mongolia is the last truly wild horse species on Earth. But for five decades it was extinct in the wild. Called *takhi*, or "spirit," in Mongolian, the horse is native to Mongolia. It fell victim to hunting and habitat loss in the early 1900s. By the 1960s, the horses were gone in the wild and found only in captivity.

In 1992, though, they returned. In a combined effort between the Mongolian Association for the Conservation of Nature and Environment and a Dutch foundation dedicated to preserving Przewalski's horse, 16 horses were brought from Europe.[8] Many others followed. The combined efforts of programs and individuals have resulted in the horse's status being upgraded from extinct in the wild to endangered.

SCIENCE CONNECTION

THE ROLE OF KEYSTONE SPECIES

All ecosystems feature intricate, interconnected systems of relationships between the environment and the species that live there. Yet scientists have determined that certain species play more critical roles in an ecosystem than others. They are called keystone species.

The first person to understand this was a professor at the University of Washington. Robert T. Paine introduced the concept in 1969 after studying the species in the intertidal zone of Washington's Pacific coast. He observed that a carnivorous starfish, *Pisaster ochraceus*, kept the populations of other species in balance. When the starfish was removed, two mussel species' populations grew unchecked because they no longer had a predator. The mussels crowded out other species, and the ecosystem's diversity decreased.

The removal of the starfish, or any keystone species, creates a chain reaction that affects many parts of the ecosystem. As with the mussels along Washington's coast, some species thrive when a keystone species is removed; other populations suffer. Plant diversity is also affected because some plants become over- or undergrazed by other species. Other examples of keystone species include wolves, beavers, alligators, and otters.

As a result of increased understanding of the role of keystone species in their ecosystems, these species have become a focus of animal conservation. Wildlife biologists can begin to stabilize an entire habitat or ecosystem by protecting keystone species.

TECHNOLOGY IN ANIMAL CONSERVATION

A computer scientist may seem like an unlikely candidate to be on the front lines of animal conservation, but increasingly technology is playing a critical role in habitat restoration, breeding, reintroduction, monitoring, and other efforts to save species. The use of technology includes data collection and analysis, artificial intelligence, radio collars, drones, and more. This is where the tech world meets the animal world in an effort to save species at risk.

Animal conservationists, including those who study Amazon river dolphins, have found drones to be useful tools in their work.

SAVING ZEBRAS

It is a well-established fact that one of the key ingredients for successful animal conservation is research. Conservationists need to understand how species interact with one another and with their environment. They need to know the threats facing a species. And they need a complete understanding of that species' natural history. In many cases, wildlife biologists trek through the wilderness to gather information. They may spend long days in the field observing or following animals. The information gathered gives them a snapshot of a population of a species. Yet advancing technology, such as artificial intelligence, can now give animal conservationists a broader snapshot of a species' overall well-being much more quickly.

In Africa, for example, zebras are on the verge of extinction. Among other factors, zebras are harmed by the increase in livestock, which pushes the zebras to marginal grazing areas and limits their access to water. To better understand any population of animals, identifying and tracking individuals is important. With zebras, though, that can be difficult. Like the fingerprints on humans, a zebra's stripes are unique to each individual. But distinguishing between two zebras'

RADIO TELEMETRY

Wildlife biologists have used radio telemetry since the 1960s as a tool to locate and track animals. The system has three parts. The first is a radio transmitter worn by the animal. It can be in the form of a collar for larger animals or a harness on a bird's back. It transmits radio signals. In the field, scientists have a radio antenna and a receiver. The antenna picks up the signals sent by the animal's radio transmitter. The radio signals picked up by the antenna are converted to a beeping noise by the receiver. As scientists get closer to an animal with a radio transmitter, the beeping gets louder, allowing them to locate the animal.

patterns to recognize an individual is time-consuming. Tanya Berger-Wolf, a professor of computer science at the University of Illinois at Chicago, helped develop a solution to that problem—a software platform called Wildbook. Using artificial intelligence, cameras, and volunteers, she is accelerating research to get a better understanding of the plight of Grevy's zebra, a critically endangered species in Kenya.

Dozens of conservation managers, individuals, government officials, and pastoral livestock owners are given cameras and two days to take pictures of zebras during the Great Grevy's Rally, a national census of the Grevy's zebras. During this time, thousands of photographs are taken and uploaded to a computer. The Wildbook algorithms then look at the pixels on a photograph, create a "map" of a zebra's stripes, compare the photo to those in archives, and determine whether it's an individual the team has seen before. If it's an animal they've seen before, they get a historical record including location and the other zebras it lives near. This database is essential to understanding the

TRACKING BUTTERFLIES

Technology is being used to track monarch butterflies, but not with drones or artificial intelligence. Instead, scientists are using an electronic tag that weighs less than a chicken feather. Fitting a butterfly with a tag is no easy task, but once it is attached, scientists can track its migration to get a better sense of its flight path and the habitats it visits along the way. The tiny device sends signals to the scientists' radio antenna either on the ground or in planes, allowing them to follow the butterfly. Knowing where the butterflies go can guide efforts to preserve the remaining habitats that monarchs depend on during migration.

In late January 2018, 212 photographers in 143 vehicles participated in the second Great Grevy's Rally. They covered 9,700 square miles (25,000 sq km) and snapped 23,000 photographs of Grevy's zebras.[1]

Thanks to technological advances, simply taking photos of zebras can be a powerful conservation tool.

population of zebras in Kenya. The technology can also be used to identify individual giraffes, turtles, elephants, and whales.

All of this information in the Wildbook is used by conservationists to inform policymakers. This may lead to the protection of important travel corridors or help convince farmers to leave a section of land fallow. As Joyce Nyaruai-Mbataru from the Kenya Wildlife Conservancies Association explained, "I think this [information] will be very helpful for us as an organization to get to know the statistics and then that will help us engage more with the government to show them whether this species are declining or they're growing, and help us to come up with a strategy on how we can conserve this species."[2]

BIOACOUSTICS

Scientists do not rely on visual data alone. They also use acoustic data. Every environment is full of sound. In natural environments, those sounds provide scientists with information about the species that live there. Conservationists use bioacoustics to supplement the visual data they have on a species or area. They use small audio recording devices, often powered by solar cells and linked to cell phone networks, to upload data. Then they eavesdrop. Once the data is collected, algorithms sort the information and provide a clear assessment of the biodiversity in an area. The technology is also helping to detect illegal deforestation in tropical rain forests, as well as the gunshots of poachers.

HIGH-TECH PROTECTION

Technology isn't just being used to monitor animals like the lynx in Colorado and condors in California and Mexico. It's also being used to track poachers. Wildlife trafficking is a billion-dollar industry. Every year, more than 20,000 African elephants are killed for their ivory tusks. Every month, 100 rhinos are killed for their horns.[3] Tigers, pangolins, and other species are also facing overexploitation at the hands of poachers and are at risk of extinction.

Unfortunately, the groups assigned to protect the areas where these species live have too large an area to patrol, too few rangers, and certainly not enough weapons. But now they have technology. Similar to the Wildbook software platform, the Spatial Monitoring and Reporting Tool (SMART) creates a database of information that helps rangers patrol more efficiently. When rangers come across signs of poachers, such as campsites, traps, or animal carcasses, they enter the location. The information is uploaded to the SMART platform. As data is collected over time, rangers identify areas where they should focus their patrols and get a clearer sense of whether their patrols have been effective.

In the past, if rangers heard a gunshot, by the time they got to the site the animal would be dead and the

Rangers in Kruger National Park use technology and training to fight back against poachers and protect animals.

poachers would be gone. Technology now allows rangers to actively target poachers and track the movement of people in and out of an area. In South Africa's Kruger National Park, a vast reserve, there is now Wi-Fi. This is linked to camera traps, fence alarms, and tracking systems. Each piece of technology communicates with other parts of the system. Rangers carry tablets that alert them to suspicious activity and provide the coordinates. Being able to act immediately is helping to save animals' lives and reduce the incidence of poaching.

OLD-FASHIONED TECHNOLOGY

Not so long ago, conservation science was anything but high tech. In the 1960s, the Galveston Laboratory of the US Bureau of Commercial Fisheries used messages in bottles to track surface currents. The 7,863 bottles were released into the Gulf of Mexico in the early 1960s to study the effects of the currents on young shrimp migrating from spawning grounds offshore to nursery grounds near shore.[4] Inside each corked bottle was a postcard. Whoever found the postcard was directed to fill it out, reporting where the bottle had been found and the date. People who returned the postcard received 50 cents. At the time, this was cutting-edge science that helped researchers discover correlations between ocean currents and species populations.

Another tool used by conservationists to track and deter poachers is drone technology. Drones can be fitted with cameras and thermal imaging sensors that allow rangers to monitor populations of animals from afar. They also spot poachers. Then rangers and local police are alerted to catch the criminals. Drones also collect data on the habits of the poachers themselves.

Drone technology is used in other areas of animal conservation as well. Drones can cover vast areas of land and sea, allowing scientists to efficiently observe and collect data on species and habitats. Moreover, drones have been found to be more accurate in counting animal populations than people. Using drones, the data scientists collect over time can help them monitor changes in species' populations as well as their habitats. Technology is giving animal conservation scientists faster and more accurate population estimates, which in turn provides stronger evidence to direct wildlife management policies. Quick action is especially important for species threatened with extinction.

Drones can do more than keep an eye on animals from above. For example, they have been used to collect whale snot. The samples were then used to analyze the whale's DNA in a noninvasive manner.

BATTLING INVASIVE SPECIES

According to the International Union for Conservation of Nature (IUCN) Red List of Threatened Species, 40 percent of amphibians are facing extinction.[1] Scientific studies have revealed that amphibian populations have been in decline for decades. In fact, more than 100 amphibian species have already gone extinct. The reasons for this include habitat loss and degradation, climate change, overexploitation, pollution, and now chytridiomycosis—a disease caused by the chytrid fungus. This infectious disease is threatening to wipe out stream-dwelling frogs around the world. In the face of this epidemic, scientists and volunteers are scrambling to save them.

Many amphibian species, including the Panamanian golden frog, are threatened.

SAVE THE FROGS

There are more than 8,000 identified species of amphibians in the world.[3]

In Panama, the Thousand Frog Stream runs near the small town of El Valle. It was so named because at one time the stream was a cacophony of noise from the thousands of frogs there. One species in particular, the golden frog, was abundant. Then, in the early 2000s, researchers began to notice a decline in the number of golden frogs and other amphibians near El Valle. Researchers in other towns reported a similar decline. By 2004, biologists from Panama and the United States understood the seriousness of the situation. To preserve the golden frog and other frog species, they planned to collect any remaining individuals they could find and raise them in captivity. Part of the plan included building a new lab facility in El Valle. But the chytrid fungus killing the frogs was moving faster than the construction of the lab. Biologists knew they couldn't wait. In 2006 and 2007, they raced to find as many frogs as they could, even though they had nowhere to house them.

Desperate, the biologists rented hotel rooms for the frogs. Edgardo Griffith, a herpetologist, and his wife went out in the evenings to catch dinner for the frogs. The hotel became fondly known as "the incredible frog hotel" with room service and round-the-clock care.[2] Every day, Griffith and his team gave the frogs antifungal baths. The surviving frogs were kept in a quarantine room until they were clear of the fungus. Then they were moved to a clean room.

Researchers and technicians help protect amphibians in a carefully controlled conservation center in Panama.

Once the El Valle Amphibian Conservation Center (EVACC) was complete, the frogs were transferred. Today, the modest facility, which is largely financed by the Houston Zoo, is full of tanks, each housing endangered frogs and other amphibians. It is completely cut off from the outside world. EVACC takes extraordinary measures to ensure that whatever is outside the facility killing amphibians stays outside. Everything that comes into the building is completely disinfected. That includes new frogs. Humans entering the building must leave behind personal belongings and wear special shoes. The water used in the tanks is also filtered and treated.

> **"Every one of them has the same value to me as an elephant."[5]**
>
> *—Edgardo Griffith, a herpetologist at EVACC in Panama, about the frogs in his care*

THE IMPORTANCE OF FROGS

Frogs are important not only to the ecosystems in which they live but also to humans. In their habitats, frogs are an interconnected part of the food web, eating a variety of insects. Some of those insects are carriers of diseases that infect people. This means that frogs help protect the human population against malaria, Lyme disease, typhoid fever, and more. In addition to being predators, frogs serve as prey to many other species. And tadpoles keep their habitats clean because they feed on algae. If frogs disappeared, entire food webs would be in jeopardy.

EVACC is considered an amphibian ark because of its mission to save a few individuals of as many species of amphibians as possible. Still, Griffith is realistic. He said, "We are losing all these amphibians before we even know that they exist."[4]

DISEASE

While Griffith and others had saved many species of amphibian from certain extinction, they still did not understand what was killing them. Then, blue poison-dart frogs at the National Zoo in Washington, DC, started dying inexplicably. Using a scanning electron microscope, a veterinary pathologist at the zoo analyzed samples from the dead frogs. He discovered a microorganism on the frogs' skin. It was a fungus that was eventually determined to be chytrid fungus. It interrupts the ability of the amphibian's skin to absorb critical substances. The amphibians ultimately die of heart failure.

Yet knowing the cause of mass amphibian fatalities has not helped scientists find a solution to saving them in the wild. The Thousand Frog Stream is now mostly quiet, aside from the trickle of water. Still, the chytrid fungi live on in the forest even after wiping out so many amphibians. A single creature can be disinfected, but entire forests cannot. And chytrid fungus continues to spread.

What scientists do know is that the spread of the fungus is the result of human activity. Through genetic analysis, researchers discovered that the origin of chytrid fungus was in East Asia. Further, the evolution of the disease coincides with the emergence of the commercial pet trade of amphibians in the 1950s. This trade spread amphibians and the disease around the world. The research also revealed that the chytrid fungus is quite diverse, and the type killing amphibians is only one of many.

Some species of amphibians are more resistant to the disease than others. And some species are showing an increased resistance. The best defense against spreading the disease further, however, is stopping the amphibian trade. It could also help prevent the spread of other strains of chytrid. But as of 2019, much of the international trade in amphibians continued.

"This is the worst pathogen in the history of the world, as far as we can tell, in terms of its impacts on biodiversity."[6]

—Mat Fisher, Imperial College of London, on the chytrid fungus

CITIZEN SCIENCE: FROGWATCH USA

In addition to professionally trained scientists, individuals are getting involved in frog conservation. In fact, scientists are calling on the public to help gather data. Volunteers for FrogWatch USA are trained to listen for both frogs and toads. Any observations and information gathered are submitted to a national online database. The data is analyzed and used to formulate strategies for frog conservation efforts across the United States.

SAVING NATIVE SPECIES

As a result of human travel around the world, new species are frequently introduced to non-native environments. The species that are not native often cause ecological harm and make an ecosystem unbalanced. They aren't always in the form of a disease like the chytrid fungus—mussels, fish, snakes, birds, hogs, plants, and more have all become invasive species. And, like the chytrid fungus, they often thrive in their new habitat to the detriment of the native species there. These species not only prey on native species but also compete against them for food, alter ecosystems, and even sicken humans.

MARINE INVASIVE SPECIES

Every ecosystem on Earth is vulnerable to invasive species. That includes marine environments. Sometime during the 1980s, the zebra mussel hitched a ride on a ship in Europe that was headed to the Great Lakes. Once the ship arrived, the mussels did well in their new environment and quickly spread. However, they have harmed the entire Great Lakes ecosystem by competing for food sources with native species and attaching themselves to native mussels. Researchers are continuing to experiment with ways to control and eradicate this invasive species.

There are many ways that conservationists help to protect native species from invasive ones. In Florida, for example, the Burmese python was introduced into the Everglades ecosystem by pet owners who either released their snakes or allowed them to escape. These snakes will eat a wide variety of animals, including deer and alligators, and have become a threat to the Everglades ecosystem. To combat this, biologists are on the lookout for pythons. Citizens are also encouraged to call when a snake is spotted so trained responders can remove it. And bounty hunters are in pursuit, paid by the state based on the size of the snake caught. These snake bounty hunters have an eye for spotting the large reptiles that are well camouflaged in the Everglades ecosystem. Hunters such as Donna Kalil scan the landscape. When she sees a python, she moves in, then nabs the snake just behind the head. Once captured, the snakes are killed humanely.

Another conservation effort to remove an invasive species is on the uninhabited Teuaua Island in French Polynesia. "This island is a critical habitat for breeding and roosting seabirds and offers a glimpse into the once-rich coastal ecosystems that existed across the Marquesas archipelago," explained project manager Tehani Withers.[7] But for a long time, non-native rats preyed on bird eggs and hatchlings, as well as on island vegetation. Scientists feared that if the rats were left unchecked, the bird populations would be decimated.

Signs posted in the Everglades warn visitors to watch out for Burmese pythons.

Conservationists took boats to the island and scrambled onto a narrow ledge. To get to the main part of the island, though, they had to use ropes to climb a 33-foot (10 m) cliff and haul their equipment to the top. Then, once they reached the top, thousands of sooty terns began dive-bombing them to protect their nests. Conservationists had to battle not only the birds but also strong winds and scorching sun to remove the invasive rats from the island. They tossed poisoned food by hand to accomplish this. At last, in 2019, the island was declared predator free. "We are optimistic seabirds once present on the island may return, increasing the diversity of the island's seabird community," says Steve Cranwell, BirdLife International Pacific Seabird Programme manager.[8]

THE DODO

A species of large, flightless bird once lived on the island of Mauritius in the southwest part of the Indian Ocean. The dodo had no predators, and it even laid its eggs right on the ground. But then a fleet of Dutch ships discovered Mauritius in 1598, and soon there was a settlement on the island. The settlers brought pigs, goats, and rats that preyed on the dodo and its eggs. Within 100 years the dodo was extinct. The extinction of the dodo was an accident, but it became a cautionary tale about the dangers of invasive species.

In the United States, the National Invasive Species Council is charged with leading strategic planning around invasive species. This includes preventing species from being introduced into non-native ecosystems, removing an entire population of an invasive species, managing invasive species to minimize impact, and restoring damaged habitats.

Understanding the history and biology of species is critical to their management. Further, sharing this information across borders is necessary as non-native species are

Sooty terns live in vast flocks on tropical islands.

moved around the world. Because of the rate of globalization, the introduction of species to new environments is unpredictable, as are the consequences of these actions. To control invasive species, therefore, requires the collaboration of scientists, governments, and private citizens. National and international policy to restrict and ban the trade of animals will help stop invasive species from being introduced in the first place. Educating the public and making people aware of the negative effects such species can have will help, too.

THE FUTURE OF ANIMAL CONSERVATION SCIENCE

Animal conservationists are responsible for saving black-footed ferrets, bald eagles, American alligators, whooping cranes, gray wolves, and many other species. Yet there is still work to do. Some extinctions occur as a natural part of life on Earth. However, in the modern world, the rate of extinction is accelerated. Some scientists warn that the rate of species loss rivals those of past mass-extinction events. Some even call the modern era the sixth mass extinction. This time there is no catastrophic natural event to blame. The extinction is caused by humans.

Bald eagles are among the species that have been helped by a combination of legislation and on-the-ground work by conservationists.

By 2019, approximately 15 percent of Earth's land and water was protected as a result of international conservation efforts.[2]

FROZEN ZOO

In the wake of this ongoing disaster, scientists have searched for innovative ways to save and preserve species. One idea involves a frozen zoo. Researchers at the San Diego Zoo's Institute for Conservation Research in California are racing to collect DNA samples from as many living species as possible. There are samples from whales, ibis, rhinos, turtles, and others. The zoo has more than 10,000 samples that represent approximately 1,000 species and subspecies in an effort to preserve what it calls "a legacy of life on Earth."[1]

Once a sample is collected, cells are grown in the lab. Then they are frozen in two different locations. Some of the samples at the zoo represent species facing extinction, such as Przewalski's horse. Other species, such as the po'ouli, a stocky Hawaiian bird, have already gone extinct.

While the efforts at the Frozen Zoo are impressive, scientists understand that to truly create a bank of

The Frozen Zoo stores samples in large stainless steel vats.

As of 2019, 25 percent of mammals and 14 percent of birds were listed on the IUCN Red List as threatened with extinction.[5]

Earth's species' DNA, a global network of frozen zoos is needed. The zoo has samples representing 1,000 species, but as of 2019 there were more than 26,000 vulnerable, critical, or endangered species in the world.[3]

DE-EXTINCTION?

Scientists have collected a wide array of DNA samples, but what can they do with them? In some ways, the Frozen Zoo is like a catalog or a museum of biodiversity. But it is also a source of research. The samples are frozen in liquid nitrogen at −321 degrees Fahrenheit (−196°C) and thawed when a researcher wants to use the sample.[4]

The samples are used to study chromosomes and evolution, gene sequencing, and genetics across subspecies. There's also hope that one day extinct species can be brought back to life using the frozen DNA. Such a feat would be known as de-extinction. The work at the Frozen Zoo sounds like something out of a science fiction film, but researchers are getting

POACHERS TURNED PROTECTORS

In many poor areas of the world, poaching is a means of income, and the needs of people's families outweigh their concerns for wildlife. In Namibia in the 1980s, an extreme drought made the local people even more desperate. Many turned to poaching. Wildlife started to disappear. Then, an organization called Integrated Rural Development and Nature Conservation (IRDNC) proposed paying people to look after the wildlife. The poachers became the protectors. IRDNC has helped not only people but also the populations of lions, black rhinos, leopards, and other species. The partnership between science and the local community has become the foundation for Namibia's conservation.

DNA sequencing may be the first step in the ultimate form of animal conservation: bringing species back from extinction.

closer to making de-extinction a reality. Using the preserved cells, scientists reprogram them into stem cells. This type of cell can, in theory, be used to re-create any type of cell in the body. The goal is to use the stem cells to create eggs and sperm of extinct or endangered species, such as the northern white rhino. The work with lab mice and other small animals has been promising. Following the death of the last male northern white rhino, Sudan, in 2018, scientists are hoping the samples they have can be used to someday generate a new population of northern white rhinos. However, a new baby northern white rhino is still something of the future. In addition, the debate about the ethics of bringing species back from extinction is heated and ongoing.

Though the last male northern white rhino has died, future technology may offer the possibility of the species' de-extinction.

PASSENGER PIGEON PROJECT

The last known passenger pigeon on Earth, Martha, died at the Cincinnati Zoo in 1914. Today, American scientist Ben Novak is working on the species' de-extinction. His desire to revive the species led him to a lab at the University of California, Santa Cruz, where scientists study the DNA of extinct animals. Novak is working to build a flock of pigeons with edited DNA from stuffed passenger pigeons in museum collections. Starting with the common rock pigeon, Novak is building a flock using gene-editing technology that allows scientists to cut and paste, adding or deleting genetic information. Novak and his team are still a long way away from adding passenger pigeon traits to the birds they are raising, but in the future Novak hopes to have a hybrid bird that resembles the extinct passenger pigeon.

WORKING HARD TO SAVE ANIMALS

Whether they are slogging through the Everglades, scuba diving through a coral farm, operating a drone, or dodging dive-bombing birds, animal conservationists around the world are working to protect animals, collect information, and raise awareness. Zebra rallies are helping to inform conservation policy. Monitoring lynx led biologists to rethink how they introduced species to increase survival rates. Tracking monarch butterfly migration routes helps direct efforts to save their migration habitats. At frog hotels, conservationists raced to save amphibians from invasive species. Raising California condor chicks using condor-shaped hand puppets will allow them to be released into the wild. Animal matchmaking ensures genetic diversity among Earth's most endangered animals. Fish climb ladders to get around dams and other barriers to return to their historic spawning grounds. And new conservation technology makes all of the work more efficient.

All of the slogging, swimming, monitoring, and collecting gives scientists a clearer understanding of ecosystems and the species that live in them, as well as human impacts on them. This knowledge is crucial in guiding action to conserve animals. Just as importantly, this information is shared with the public to raise awareness. Many of the effects humans have had on animals arose from ignorance—people simply didn't understand how their actions would harm entire species or how individual choices can have global impacts. This knowledge empowers individuals to be part of conservation efforts. Animal conservationists may be on the front line in caves, oceans, rain forests, and everywhere in between, but this work relies on ongoing partnerships between scientists, individuals, governments, local officials, and conservation groups.

THERE'S AN APP FOR THAT

The future of animal conservation science relies on professionally trained scientists as well as on citizen scientists. Mobile technology has opened up opportunities for citizens to learn about wildlife conservation efforts and to be a part of them. For example, citizens can determine changes in bird distribution throughout the seasons using the eBird app by submitting photos that are then analyzed by scientists. This kind of data collection has always been a foundation of animal conservation, and today crowdsourced data collection is playing an increasingly important role. Not only does it increase the number of people in the field but it can also be a more efficient use of research funding.

"Only if we understand, will we care. Only if we care, will we help. Only if we help, shall all be saved."[6]

—Jane Goodall, scientist and conservationist

ESSENTIAL FACTS

SIGNIFICANT EVENTS

▸ Rachel Carson's *Silent Spring* was published in 1962. The book raised awareness about the effects of the pesticide DDT on bird populations and initiated the modern environmental movement.

▸ In 1973, the Endangered Species Act was signed into law by President Richard Nixon, creating protections for species of plants and animals threatened with extinction.

▸ Zoos and aquariums shifted from acquiring wild animals to breeding animals in captivity in the 1970s. These programs, which include animal matchmaking, serve to increase the population of declining species with a focus on genetic diversity.

▸ El Valle Amphibian Conservation Center (EVACC) was completed in Panama in the early 2000s and serves as an amphibian ark for amphibians facing extinction as a result of the deadly, invasive chytrid fungus.

KEY PLAYERS

▸ Rachel Carson was a biologist and author whose exhaustive scientific work uncovered the effects of the pesticide DDT on the environment. Her book *Silent Spring* led to a shift in the role of science from conquering and controlling nature to helping to preserve it.

▸ Ken Nedimyer, founder of the Coral Restoration Foundation, is actively restoring coral reefs around Florida by cultivating corals in coral nurseries and then replanting them on carefully selected reef sites.

- Tanya Berger-Wolf, a professor of computer science at the University of Illinois at Chicago, helped develop a software platform called Wildbook. This platform integrates wildlife research, citizen scientists, artificial intelligence, and computers to more efficiently and effectively analyze species populations in order to combat extinction.

- The US Fish and Wildlife Service is the US agency charged with managing protected areas and protecting endangered species and migratory birds; offices around the country are involved in countless projects to conserve wildlife.

- The National Oceanic and Atmospheric Administration (NOAA) uses science, service, and stewardship to conserve coastal and marine ecosystems; to that end, NOAA has completed more than 600 fish migration projects to recover fish populations around the United States.

IMPACT ON SCIENCE

Following the publication of *Silent Spring* in 1962, the role of science shifted from conquering and controlling nature to preserving and protecting it. This initiated the modern environmental movement and the development of conservation science. Animal conservation since that time has grown and changed, with knowledge building from one project or program to the next since each animal and each ecosystem is unique. Today's conservationists use best practices, exhaustive data collection, solid science, and the latest innovations to guide action to save species at risk. All of this work builds knowledge, and partnered with the efforts of other conservationists, individuals, groups, local and federal officials, and policymakers, it is saving species.

QUOTE

"We must begin to count the many hidden costs of what we are doing."

—*Rachel Carson*

GLOSSARY

algorithm
A set of steps followed to solve a mathematical problem or to complete a computer process.

artificial intelligence
The use of computer technology to simulate human intelligence.

biodiversity
The variety of species in a given area.

conservation
Purposeful, planned preservation and protection of wildlife and their habitats from exploitation or destruction.

degradation
The process of damaging or destroying an ecosystem.

ecosystem
A community of interacting organisms and their environment.

entomologist
A scientist who studies insects.

fallow
Left intentionally unused during the growing season.

genetic diversity
The variety of genes within a population of a species.

geneticist

A biologist who studies heredity and variations of species that are controlled by genes.

globalization

The movement toward a world more connected by trade, finance, and communications.

habitat fragmentation

The division of large, connected ecosystems into smaller, disconnected, and isolated sections.

herpetologist

A scientist who studies reptiles and amphibians.

hydrology

The science of how water moves with respect to the land around it.

indicator species

Species whose overall population and status can reveal information about the changes in, and health of, an ecosystem.

invasive species

An organism that arrives in a new ecosystem, takes over, and causes harm.

poaching

The illegal taking of wild animals.

trafficking

Dealing or trading in something illegal.

ADDITIONAL RESOURCES

SELECTED BIBLIOGRAPHY

Carson, Rachel. *Silent Spring*. Houghton Mifflin, 1962. Print.

National Park Service. US Department of the Interior, n.d., nps.gov. Accessed 18 Feb. 2019.

Roman, Joe. *Listed: Dispatches from America's Endangered Species Act*. Harvard UP, 2011. Print.

Titlow, Budd, and Mariah Tinger. *Protecting the Planet: Environmental Champions from Conservation to Climate Change*. Prometheus Books, 2016. Print.

US Fish & Wildlife Service. US Department of the Interior, n.d., fws.gov. Accessed 14 Feb. 2019.

FURTHER READINGS

Amstutz, Lisa J. *Bringing Back Our Freshwater Lakes*. Minneapolis: Abdo, 2018. Print.

Hand, Carol. *Bringing Back Our Tropical Forests*. Minneapolis: Abdo, 2018. Print.

MacCarald, Clara. *Bringing Back Our Deserts*. Minneapolis: Abdo, 2018. Print.

Perdew, Laura. *Bringing Back Our Wetlands*. Minneapolis: Abdo, 2018. Print.

ONLINE RESOURCES

To learn more about animal conservationists, please visit **abdobooklinks.com** or scan this QR code. These links are routinely monitored and updated to provide the most current information available.

MORE INFORMATION

For more information on this subject, contact or visit the following organizations:

AMERICAN MUSEUM OF NATURAL HISTORY
Central Park West at Seventy-Ninth St.
New York, NY 10024-5192
212-769-5100
amnh.org/about-the-museum
The American Museum of Natural History's mission is to discover and share information about the natural world. It is world renowned for its exhibits and scientific collections.

SOUTHWEST WILDLIFE CONSERVATION CENTER
27026 N. 156th St.
Scottsdale, AZ 85262
480-471-9109
southwestwildlife.org
The Southwest Wildlife Conservation Center rescues, rehabilitates, and releases injured wildlife. Animals that cannot be released are given sanctuary at the center. Visits are by appointment only.

WONDERS OF WILDLIFE NATIONAL MUSEUM AND AQUARIUM
500 W. Sunshine St.
Springfield, MO 65807
888-222-6060
wondersofwildlife.org
Opened in 2017, this museum and aquarium is dedicated to sparking wonder and paying tribute to America's conservation movement.

SOURCE NOTES

CHAPTER 1. RACING TO SAVE BATS

1. "Bat." *San Diego Zoo Animals & Plants*, n.d., animals.sandiegozoo.org. Accessed 13 Mar. 2019.

2. Alina Bradford. "Bats: Fuzzy Flying Mammals." *Live Science*, 24 Oct. 2018, livescience.com. Accessed 27 Feb. 2019.

3. Jim Robbins. "Saving the Bats, One Cave at a Time." *New York Times*, 18 Feb. 2019, nytimes.com. Accessed 27 Feb. 2019.

4. "New Hope for Bats." *Nature Conservancy*, n.d., nature.org. Accessed 27 Feb. 2019.

5. Cristián Samper. "Science: The Key to Wildlife Conservation." *Huff Post*, 22 Apr. 2017, huffingtonpost.com. Accessed 27 Feb. 2019.

6. Robbins, "Saving the Bats, One Cave at a Time."

CHAPTER 2. THE HISTORY OF ANIMAL CONSERVATION

1. Lawrence Downing. "John Muir and the United States National Park System." *Sierra Club*, 2019, sierraclub.org. Accessed 25 July 2019.

2. "Time Line of the American Bison." *US Fish & Wildlife Service*, n.d., fws.gov. Accessed 14 Feb. 2019.

3. Joe Roman. *Listed: Dispatches from America's Endangered Species Act*. Harvard UP, 2011. 17.

4. "Quotations from John Muir." *Sierra Club*, 2019, sierraclub.org. Accessed 24 June 2019.

5. Budd Titlow and Mariah Tinger. *Protecting the Planet: Environmental Champions from Conservation to Climate Change*. Prometheus, 2016. 125–127.

6. "Background and History." *IUCN Red List*, n.d., iucnredlist.org. Accessed 18 Mar. 2019.

7. "The Passenger Pigeon." *Smithsonian*, Mar. 2001, si.edu. Accessed 12 Feb. 2019.

8. "American Experience: Rachel Carson, Chapter 1." *YouTube*, 1 Jan. 2017, youtube.com. Accessed 17 Feb. 2019.

9. "Fact Sheet: Natural History, Ecology, and History of Recovery." *US Fish & Wildlife Service*, 4 Mar. 2019, fws.gov. Accessed 13 Mar. 2019.

10. "Advancing Science in the Endangered Species Act—A Toolkit for Scientists." *Center for Science and Democracy*, July 2017, ucsa.org. Accessed 13 Mar. 2019.

11. "Advancing Science in the Endangered Species Act."

CHAPTER 3. SAVING HABITATS, SAVING SPECIES

1. "Size and Interconnectedness." *Friends of the Everglades*, n.d., everglades.org. Accessed 25 June 2019.

2. "Restoration of Everglades National Park," *National Park Service*, n.d., nps.gov. Accessed 25 June 2019.

3. "United States of America, North America." *Protected Planet*, Mar. 2019, protectedplanet.net. Accessed 14 Mar. 2019.

4. "Analysis of US MPAs." *Marine Protected Areas*, n.d., marineprotectedareas.noaa.gov. Accessed 14 Mar. 2019.

5. "American Alligator Ecology and Monitoring for the Comprehensive Everglades Restoration Plan." *USGS*, 18 Feb. 2014, pubs.usgs.gov. Accessed 14 Mar. 2019.

6. Joe Roman. *Listed: Dispatches from America's Endangered Species Act*. Harvard UP, 2011. 91–92.

7. "Monarch Conservation." *Xerces Society*, n.d., xerces.org. Accessed 1 Mar. 2019.

8. Giorgia Guglielmi. "Protecting Monarch Butterflies Could Mean Moving Hundreds of Trees." *Scientific American*, 22 Jan. 2019, scientificamerican.com. Accessed 25 June 2019.

9. Guglielmi, "Protecting Monarch Butterflies."

CHAPTER 4. BREEDING AND REHABILITATION

1. "California Condor Reintroduction & Recovery." *National Park Service*, 25 Jan. 2017, nps.gov. Accessed 3 Mar. 2019.

2. "California Condor Recovery Program." *US Fish and Wildlife Service-Pacific Southwest Region*, 6 Nov. 2018, fws.gov. Accessed 3 Mar. 2019.

3. "About the Rocky Mountain Raptor Program." *RMRP*, 2019, rmrp.org. Accessed 25 June 2019.

4. "California Condor Reintroduction & Recovery."

5. Larry B. Stammer. "First Captive California Condors Freed in Wild." *Los Angeles Times*, 15 Jan. 1992, latimes.com. Accessed 25 June 2019.

6. "California Condor Recovery Program."

7. David DeMille. "Push Made to Prevent Lead Poisoning in California Condors, Other Animals." *Spectrum*, 28 Nov. 2017, thespectrum.com. Accessed 25 June 2019.

8. "Captive Breeding Success Stories." *Nature*, 1 Apr. 2009, pbs.org. Accessed 5 Mar. 2019.

9. Leslie Stahl. "Matchmaking for Zoo Animals." *60 Minutes*, 13 May 2019, cbsnews.com. Accessed 5 Mar. 2019.

CHAPTER 5. AQUATIC BREEDING

1. "Coral Reefs 101." *National Geographic*, 2017, video.nationalgeographic.com. Accessed 21 Feb. 2019.

2. "Coral Reefs 101."

3. "Restoration." *Coral Restoration Foundation*, 2018, coralrestoration.org. Accessed 21 Feb. 2019.

4. "Coral Restoration Foundation." *Vimeo*, 2012, vimeo.com. Accessed 25 June 2019.

5. "Restoration."

6. "Restoration."

7. "Seeding the Keys: The Coral Restoration Foundation." *Vimeo*, 2011, vimeo.com. Accessed 25 June 2019.

8. "Successful Fish Passage Efforts across the Nation." *NOAA Fisheries*, 16 Apr. 2018, fisheries.noaa.gov. Accessed 25 June 2019.

9. "Reopening Rivers for Migratory Fish." *NOAA Fisheries*, 10 Aug. 2018, fisheries.noaa.gov. Accessed 25 June 2019.

10. "Reopening Rivers for Migratory Fish."

SOURCE NOTES CONTINUED

CHAPTER 6. REINTRODUCTION

1. Rick Kahn. Personal interview. 25 Mar. 2016.

2. Tanya Shenk. "Wildlife Research Report." *Colorado Parks and Wildlife*, 2007, cpw.state.co.us. Accessed 15 Mar. 2019.

3. "Lynx Update." *Colorado Parks and Wildlife*, 25 May 2009, cpw.state.co.us. Accessed 14 Mar. 2019.

4. Nadine Siak. "David Soileau: Bringing the Louisiana Black Bear Back from the Brink." *US Fish and Wildlife Service*, 10 Mar. 2016, fws.gov. Accessed 27 Feb. 2019.

5. Joe Roman. *Listed: Dispatches from America's Endangered Species Act*. Harvard UP, 2011. 154.

6. Jennifer Errick. "9 Wildlife Success Stories." *National Parks Conservation Association*, 2 Nov. 2015, npca.org. Accessed 14 Mar. 2019.

7. Harry Cockburn. "Beavers Returned to Forest of Dean 400 Years after Being Driven to Extinction." *Independent*, 24 July 2018, independent.co.uk. Accessed 27 Feb. 2019.

8. "From Extinction to Free Ranging by Successful Reintroduction." *IUCN*, 26 Mar. 2018. Accessed 14 Mar. 2019.

CHAPTER 7. TECHNOLOGY IN ANIMAL CONSERVATION

1. Daniel Rubenstein et al. "The Great Grevy's Rally." *Grevy's Zebra Trust*, 23 June 2018, grevyszebratrust.org. Accessed 7 Mar. 2019.

2. Lisa Lahde. "This Wildlife Conservation Group Is Saving Zebras from Extinction with AI." *Forbes*, 2 May 2018, forbes.com. Accessed 7 Mar. 2019.

3. Matt Reynolds. "The War against Animal Poaching Will Be Won by Data, Not Drones." *Wired*, 11 Feb. 2018, wired.co.uk. Accessed 7 Mar. 2019.

4. Jessica Leigh Hester. "Found: A 50-Year-Old Scientific Message, Stuffed in a Bottle." *Atlas Obscura*, 18 Feb. 2019, atlasobscura.com. Accessed 7 Mar. 2019.

CHAPTER 8. BATTLING INVASIVE SPECIES

1. "The IUCN Red List of Threatened Species." *IUCN*, n.d., iucnredlist.org. Accessed 18 Mar. 2019.

2. William Booth. "Scientists Try to Save the Frogs as Time Runs Out." *Washington Post*, 30 Dec. 2012, washingtonpost.com. Accessed 9 Mar. 2019.

3. "Species by the Numbers." *Amphibiaweb*, n.d., amphibiaweb.org. Accessed 25 June 2019.

4. Elizabeth Kolbert. "The Sixth Extinction: An Unnatural History—Read an Excerpt." *Elizabeth Kolbert*, 11 Feb. 2014, elizabethkolbert.com. Accessed 9 Mar. 2019.

5. Kolbert, "The Sixth Extinction."

6. Michael Greshko. "Ground Zero of Amphibian 'Apocalypse' Finally Found." *National Geographic*, 10 May 2018, news.nationalgeographic.com. Accessed 9 Mar. 2019.

7. Jessica Law. "Momentous Mission: First Successful Invasive Species Removal in Marquesas." *Bird Life International*, 13 Feb. 2019, birdlife.org. Accessed 25 June 2019.

8. Law, "Momentous Mission."

CHAPTER 9. THE FUTURE OF ANIMAL CONSERVATION SCIENCE

1. Zach Baron. "Inside the Frozen Zoo That Could Bring Extinct Animals Back to Life." *GQ*, 27 Oct. 2016, gq.com. Accessed 12 Mar. 2019.

2. Dan Kraus. "Ten Good News Nature Conservation Stories from 2018: Our Collective Actions Can Have a Big Impact." *Nature Conservancy Canada*, 11 Jan. 2019, natureconservancy.ca. Accessed 12 Mar. 2019.

3. Amber Dance. "San Diego's Frozen Zoo Offers Hope for Endangered Species around the World." *Smithsonian*, 16 Jan. 2019, smithsonianmag.com. Accessed 12 Mar. 2019.

4. Dance, "San Diego's Frozen Zoo."

5. "Background and History." *IUCN*, n.d., iucnredlist.org. Accessed 18 Mar. 2019.

6. Marc Bekoff, PhD, "Jane Goodall: Iconic Conservationist and Pillar of Hope." *Psychology Today*, 29 Oct. 2017, psychologytoday.com. Accessed 25 June 2019.

INDEX

American alligators, 18, 27, 30, 68, 86, 90

Anthropocene era, 19

Austin, Texas, 8

bald eagle, 15–18, 22, 90

bats, 4–8, 10

beavers, 61, 66, 68

Berger-Wolf, Tanya, 73

bioacoustics, 75

biomagnification, 22

bison, 14

black bears, 64

Burmese python, 86

California condors, 36–44, 75, 98

Canada lynx, 58–64, 75, 98

captive breeding, 34, 38–39, 41, 42, 46

Carson, Rachel, 15, 16–18

chimpanzees, 92

chytrid fungus, 80, 84–86

citizen science, 6, 85, 99

climate change, 9, 24, 33, 34, 48, 80

Colorado, 38, 58–64, 75

Comprehensive Everglades Restoration Plan (CERP), 27–29, 30–31

coral reefs, 48–55

Coral Restoration Foundation (CRF), 50–55

coral transplants, 50–53

Cousteau, Jacques, 53

Cranwell, Steve, 88

Cuvier, Georges, 14

DDT, 16–17, 22

de-extinction, 94–97, 98

DNA, 10, 46, 63, 79, 92, 94, 98

dodo, 88

Douglas, Marjory Stoneman, 27

drones, 70, 78–79, 98

El Valle Amphibian Conservation Center (EVACC), 83–84

elephants, 10, 14, 75, 84

Emerson, Ralph Waldo, 12

Endangered Species Act (ESA), 18–21

Everglades, 26–33, 86–87, 98

extinction, 10, 14, 15, 39, 64, 66, 72, 76, 79, 80, 84, 88, 90–92, 94–97

Fauna Project, 29, 30

Fish and Wildlife Service, US, 15, 38, 44, 61, 64

fish ladders, 56–57

fish migration, 55–57

forensic genetics, 44

Forest Service, US, 8, 61

frogs, 44, 80–85, 98

Frozen Zoo, 92–97

genetic diversity, 39, 42, 44, 46, 52–53, 98

genetic matchmaking, 42–44, 46, 98

Georgia State University, 8

Goodall, Jane, 92, 99

Great Barrier Reef, 50

Great Grevy's Rally, 73

Griffith, Edgardo, 82, 84

habitat fragmentation, 26

Haeckel, Ernst, 15

Hamber, Jan, 41

Holliday, Cory, 7

Hornaday, William Temple, 14

Integrated Rural Development and Nature Conservation (IRDNC), 94

International Union for Conservation of Nature (IUCN), 15, 80, 94

invasive species, 6, 9, 10, 18, 66, 86–89, 98

Kenya, 73–75

keystone species, 30, 68

Kruger National Park, 78

Lacy, Bob, 42
Lawless, Amanda, 42
lead poisoning, 38
Lincoln Park Zoo, 42
Los Angeles Zoo, 38–39
lynx reintroduction, 58–64

manatees, 18, 52
milkweed, 34
monarch butterflies, 33–35, 73, 98
Moore, Joseph Curtis, 52
Muir, John, 12, 14

Namibia, 94
National Invasive Species
    Council, 88
National Oceanic and Atmospheric
    Administration (NOAA), 56–57
National Park Service, 15, 61
National Zoo, 84
Nedimyer, Ken, 50–53
Nixon, Richard, 18
northern white rhino, 97
Novak, Ben, 98
Nyaruai-Mbataru, Joyce, 75

oyamel firs, 33–35

Paine, Robert T., 68
Panama, 82, 84
passenger pigeons, 16, 18, 98
poaching, 75–76, 78, 94
pollinator gardens, 34
po'ouli, 92
Przewalski's horse, 67, 92
pupfish, 66–67

radio telemetry, 72
Rocky Mountain Raptor Program
    (RMRP), 38
Roosevelt, Theodore, 15

Sáenz-Romero, Cuauhtémoc,
    34–35
San Diego Wild Animal Park, 38
San Diego Zoo, 92
Sierra Club, 12, 14
Silent Spring, 15–18
Soileau, David, 64
sooty terns, 88
Spatial Monitoring and Reporting
    Tool (SMART), 76

Teuaua Island, 87
Thoreau, Henry David, 12
Thousand Frog Stream, 82, 84

underwater noise pollution, 55

whale earwax, 56
white-nose syndrome, 6–8, 9
Wildbook, 73–76
Withers, Tehani, 87

Yellowstone, 12, 27, 64, 66
Yosemite, 12

zebra mussel, 86
zebras, 72–75, 98

ABOUT THE AUTHOR

Laura Perdew is a mom, author, writing consultant, and self-admitted tree hugger. She began writing about conservation in sixth grade, and as an adult, she's written more than 20 books for the education market, including books on animal rights, wetland conservation, biodiversity, extinction, and renewable energy. Laura lives and plays in Boulder, Colorado.